TEACHING ADULTS

An ESL Resource Book

New Readers Press
ProLiteracy's publishing division

Acknowledgments

Many people shared in the development and production of the first edition of this book. Suzanne Abrams, Linda Church, and Tom Mueller did the research, writing, and editing; Paula Schlusberg served as ESL consultant and advisor; and Louise Damen contributed many of the ideas shared in "Communicating Across Cultures."

Many of the specific activities in the book are adapted from ideas developed by teachers and tutors who have had extensive experience working with ESL students. Their contributions are acknowledged within the text.

Vanessa Caceres updated the content in this second edition of *Teaching Adults: An ESL Resource Book*, and Lynne Weintraub contributed helpful comments.

Several activities in this book have been adapted from *Notebook: Resources for the Adult Educator*, a membership publication put out by ProLiteracy three times a year. Archived issues can be explored at **http://www.proliteracy.org/notebook.**

Teaching Adults: An ESL Resource Book, Second Edition
ISBN 978-1-56420-344-1

Copyright © 2013, 1996 New Readers Press
New Readers Press
ProLiteracy's Publishing Division
104 Marcellus Street, Syracuse, New York 13204
www.newreaderspress.com

Printed in the United States of America
9 8 7 6 5 4 3 2 1

Proceeds from the sale of New Readers Press materials support professional development, training, and technical assistance programs of ProLiteracy that benefit local literacy programs in the U.S. and around the globe.

Editor: Beth Oddy
Design and Production Director: James Wallace
Production Specialist: Maryellen Casey
Senior Designer: Carolyn Wallace

Contents

1 Introduction 7

English as a Second Language: The Challenge of Change (p. 7)

This Book (p. 10)

ProLiteracy (p. 11)

2 Language Learning 13

The Four Basic Language Skills (p. 13)

The Functions of Language (p. 14)

Second Language Acquisition (p. 15)

Becoming a Better Language Teacher (p. 21)

3 Communicating Across Cultures 23

Language Learning and Culture Learning (p. 24)

Individual Responses to Universal Situations (p. 25)

Being an Effective Culture Guide (p. 28)

4 Getting to Know Students 30

Needs Assessment (p. 30)

    Activity 1: Setting Goals (p. 32)

    Activity 2: The Language Wheel (p. 34)

Skills Assessment (p. 35)

Learning Styles and Multiple Intelligences (p. 38)

5 Listening and Speaking 40

Guidelines for Teaching Oral Skills (p. 40)

Introducing New Vocabulary (p. 42)

Total Physical Response (TPR) (p. 43)

    Activity 3: Basic Steps for TPR (p. 44)

    Activity 4: Foam Balls (p. 46)

Vocabulary Drills (p. 46)

    Activity 5: Vocabulary Drill to Teach Direction Words (p. 47)

Reinforcing Vocabulary (p. 48)

    Activity 6: Eating Utensils (p. 49)

    Activity 7: Focused Listening/Listening to a Story (p. 51)

    Activity 8: Dictation for Listening Skills (p. 52)

Idioms (p. 52)

    Activity 9: Writing a Conversation to Teach Idioms (p. 53)

Grammar (p. 54)

    Activity 10: Substitution Drills (p. 56)

    Activity 11: If I Won the Lottery (p. 57)

Conversation (p. 58)

    Activity 12: Dialogues—Basic Steps (p. 59)

    Activity 13: Role Plays (p. 62)

    Activity 14: Using Picture Stories for Health Literacy (p. 63)

    Activity 15: Conversation Prompts (p. 66)

    Activity 16: Newspapers as a Cultural Key (p. 70)

    Activity 17: Role Play—Finding an Apartment (p. 71)

Conversation Activities for Small Groups and Classes (p. 73)

    Activity 18: Question Strips (p. 73)

    Activity 19: Find Someone Who... (p. 75)

    Activity 20: Who Am I? (p. 77)

    Activity 21: "Liars" (p. 78)

    Activity 22: What's Missing? (p. 79)

    Activity 23: Meeting and Greeting—Conversation Practice (p. 81)

The Sounds of English (p. 83)

Teaching Individual Sounds (p. 84)

    Activity 24: Minimal Pairs (p. 86)

6 Reading and Writing **89**

Literacy Skills—Where Do Your Students Fit? (p. 89)

Principles of Teaching Reading and Writing (p. 90)

Language Experience Approach (p. 93)

    Activity 25: Creating a Language Experience Story (p. 94)

    Activity 26: Building Skills with LEA Stories (p. 96)

Pre-Reading Activities (p. 97)

    Activity 27: Pre-Reading Activity—Discussion (p. 98)

Recognizing Words (p. 99)

    Activity 28: Sight Words (p. 100)

    Activity 29: Phonics—Teaching Consonant Sounds (p. 101)

    Activity 30: Word Patterns (p. 102)

    Activity 31: Context—Cloze Procedure (p. 104)

    Activity 32: Word Parts—Compound Words (p. 105)

Developing Fluent Oral Reading (p. 106)

    Activity 33: Reading Aloud to Students (p. 106)

    Activity 34: Duet Reading (p. 107)

    Activity 35: Echo Reading (p. 109)

    Activity 36: Using the SQ3R Reading Approach (p. 109)

Getting Started with Writing (p. 112)

    Activity 37: Letter Formation—Five Steps to Printing (p. 113)

Guided Writing (p. 117)

    Activity 38: Sentence Completion with Pictures (p. 118)

    Activity 39: Using Pictures in One-to-One Tutoring (p. 119)

    Activity 40: Using Pictures with Small Groups (p. 121)

    Activity 41: Getting and Giving Health Information (p. 124)

    Activity 42: Using Craigslist to Sell Goods and Services (p. 124)

    Activity 43: Li's Morning Routine (p. 128)

Free Writing (p. 130)

    Activity 44: Semantic Webs (p. 130)

    Activity 45: Five-Minute Warm-Up (p. 132)

    Activity 46: "I Like to Eat Chocolate" (p. 132)

    Activity 47: Writing with Partners (p. 134)

    Activity 48: Adding Sensory Details to Autobiographical Writing (p. 137)

    Activity 49: Dialogue Journals (p. 141)

7   Integrated Communication Activities **143**

Information Grids (p. 143)

    Activity 50: Basic Steps (p. 144)

    Activity 51: Information Grids to Meet Real-Life Needs (p. 149)

    Activity 52: Information Grids to Review and Reinforce Specific Grammatical Structures or Vocabulary (p. 150)

    Activity 53: Information Grids in One-to-One Tutoring (p. 151)

Information Gap (p. 152)

    Activity 54: Supermarket Ad (p. 153)

    Activity 55: Venn Diagram (p. 155)

Other Integrated Communication Activities (p. 158)

    Activity 56: "I'm a Banana. What Are You?" (p. 158)

    Activity 57: Teaching Basic Computer Use (p. 159)

Suggestions for Additional Activities (p. 162)

8   Pulling It All Together: Lesson Planning................................ **163**

Two Ingredients of a Lesson Plan (p. 163)

Steps in Lesson Planning (p. 164)

    Step 1: Ask *Who?* (p. 164)

    Step 2: Ask *What?* (p. 166)

    Step 3: Ask *How?* (p. 166)

    Step 4: Write the Lesson Plan (p. 167)

Sample of Completed Lesson Plan Activity Sheet (p. 169)

Lesson Plan Activity Sheet (p. 171)

Appendix A: The Sounds of English.. **172**

Appendix B: Considering Assessment....................................... **178**

Introduction

English as a Second Language: The Challenge of Change

Imagine what it would be like to arrive in the United States and be unable to understand, speak, read, or write English. You would not only have to struggle with basic communication, but you would also have to learn to understand the different culture, customs, and behavior of your new neighbors.

The number of people trying to meet this challenge has grown dramatically in recent years. In 2006 there were 37.5 million foreign-born residents in the United States, or 12.5% of the total U.S. population. That's a 10.4% increase from 2000. Although numbers in states well known for immigrant populations (such as California, Texas, New York, and Florida) continue to grow, other states have also seen an unexpected surge in foreign-born residents. In fact, since 2005, 14 states experienced a 30% or greater increase. Those statistics come from the Center for Applied Linguistics (CAL) publication *Education for adult English language learners in the United States: Trends, research, and promising practices* (2010, Washington, D.C.).

The impact of this growth has been especially noticeable in urban areas and among the most disadvantaged populations. This situation is of particular concern to employers. Increasing numbers of people in the pool of potential employees are classified as "limited English proficient" and in need of English as a second language (ESL) instruction.

The ESL population in the United States is diverse in terms of country of origin, education, and individual skill levels. In addition to Mexico and other Latin American countries, a growing number of non-native speakers of English come from China, the Philippines, India, Vietnam, Korea, Eastern Europe, and African countries. There are growing enclaves from war-torn countries such as Afghanistan and Iraq. Of these residents born outside the United States, 68% have a high school diploma. The percentage that works in the civilian labor force grew 76% from 1990 to 2002, the CAL publication reports.

The new arrivals include groups with widely differing skill levels:

- Some come from countries with strong literacy traditions and are likely to be literate in their native languages.

- Some are literate in their native languages but are unfamiliar with the Roman alphabet.

- Others are unable to read or write in any language because they come from societies that provide limited educational opportunities or that only recently developed a written language.

Some of the people who are entering ESL programs are encountering English for the first time. Others have been in the United States long enough to have acquired some basic listening and speaking skills, but they are unable to read or write the language. Still others studied English in their native countries and are somewhat proficient in reading and writing English but are unable to speak or understand it.

New arrivals are faced not only with having to learn a new language but also with having to adapt to U.S. culture. For some, that is relatively easy. For others, it can be a major frustration and one that can affect their ability to function effectively both in and out of the classroom.

When you choose to work with ESL students, you will be confronted with many different needs and challenges. You will also experience the satisfaction of helping people gain the skills and information they need to meet their personal goals.

Teaching Trends

ESL tutoring and teaching have changed a great deal since the original publication of *Teaching Adults: An ESL Resource Book*. One obvious change is a greater emphasis on technology-related skills. Nowadays, tutors help students not only with listening, speaking, reading, and writing but also with using computers, smartphones, the Internet, GPS devices, and other technology both to learn English and to enhance survival skills. Learning how to use this technology can help students reach their educational and workplace goals.

Another change within ESL instruction is a stronger emphasis on teaching civics, whether at a community level (such as helping students get involved with school- or community-level projects) or at a national level (such as teaching students about upcoming elections or encouraging eligible students to register to vote). Recent changes to the U.S. citizenship test format and content have caused a greater need for citizenship-related English instruction.

Transitions to post-secondary education and the workplace play a stronger role in ESL and general adult basic education instruction now. Although many adult ESL lessons still focus on the always-needed "survival English," lessons that bridge

English instruction to future education or workplace goals are common. These lessons may include helping students write résumés, prepare for job interviews, or learn to take notes in academic classes.

More programs are using (or are required by their state to use) content standards. In short, content standards list what students should know and be able to do in a specific subject. For example, a content standard for a low-intermediate-level ESL student might be "Select appropriate questions to ask during a job interview." A content standard for a high-beginning ESL student might be "Fill out a library card form." Somewhat related to the growth in content standards is the growing trend toward assessment. For various reasons, we need to be able to qualitatively or quantitatively show instructional gains.

Although ESL instruction has changed greatly in a short period of time, one thing that has remained the same is the need for effective lessons that help students develop skills they can use outside the classroom.

The Rewards of ESL Tutoring

When you choose to work with ESL students, you will be confronted with many different needs and challenges. You will also experience the satisfaction of helping people meet their personal goals. If you listen closely, you will discover how much you have touched the lives of your students.

One Tutor's Story

Jean-Pierre was the very first ESL learner I worked with after I finished the tutor workshop. He was a 35-year-old carpenter who came to the United States from Haiti seeking political asylum. When I first met him, he could carry on only a rudimentary conversation in English. He had been to school for a few years in Haiti, so he could read and write some French. Haitian Creole was his native language.

Jean-Pierre and I agreed to meet twice a week at the neighborhood library. Although I was nervous at first, we got off to a pretty good start. We seemed to get along quite well. Jean-Pierre's main goal was to learn enough English to start his own business as a carpenter or builder.

One Saturday morning, after we had been meeting for about two weeks, we had a particularly fruitful lesson. We practiced a dialogue and did a follow-up role play to reinforce some language skills we had worked on earlier. By the end of the role play, I could tell that Jean-Pierre was feeling more comfortable with those skills. At his request, we spent the rest of the lesson working on the English he would need to buy some new tools.

After the lesson, as we were walking down the back stairs to leave the library, Jean-Pierre unexpectedly said to me, "When I come this country—

afraid. Maybe no learn English. I pray and pray every day. And now—God send you to me."

I was stunned. When I decided to try ESL tutoring, I wasn't really sure what to expect. Now, quite suddenly, the real impact of what I was doing hit home. The training I had gone through, the lesson plans I had worked on, the picture files, the teaching materials, and the activities I was developing—all of this had not prepared me for the most obvious thing: that I would not simply be teaching speaking, listening, reading, and writing in this new role of ESL tutor. I would also be making a profound impact on someone else's life.

This Book

Teaching Adults: An ESL Resource Book was developed to help you meet the needs of people like Jean-Pierre. It includes important background information on language acquisition, adult learning, and cross-cultural issues as well as specific teaching techniques and activities that can be used with a variety of students. *Teaching Adults: An ESL Resource Book* is specifically geared toward ESL tutors in a one-to-one setting, but we also provide some activities for small groups or classrooms. When there are small-group activities, we try to suggest ways they could also be used in a one-to-one setting.

The material in this book is based on the following principles:

Each adult is a unique individual.
Adult students bring a wealth of knowledge and experience to the learning process. Each student is a unique individual with his or her own needs and interests. These ideas are at the core of teaching adults. To ensure success, the tutor or teacher must work with each student to tailor the program to his or her needs and goals.

Instruction must be useful and relevant.
People learn best when they know they will be able to use their new skills and information to meet everyday needs outside the classroom. Because of this, tutors and teachers must use teaching activities—such as those included in this book—that incorporate authentic English in real-world contexts. Students should leave every session with at least one new idea or skill that they can put to immediate use.

Tutoring is effective.
It takes all kinds of programs working together to meet the diverse needs of ESL students in this country. Volunteer tutors are important partners

in that effort. By working in one-to-one or small-group settings, tutors can often provide the individualized attention that may not be available in larger classes. Well-trained tutors assess needs, select appropriate instructional materials and activities, and develop lesson plans that help students reach their goals.

Errors are a natural part of the language learning process.
People learn best when they are encouraged to communicate without worrying about making mistakes. ESL tutors and teachers must create frequent opportunities for students to share ideas and information as best they can with the English they have learned. During such times, tutors should allow students—especially beginners—to concentrate on content and not be overly concerned with grammatical correctness. When a student makes errors, the tutor or teacher should simply note these and plan to work on them later. As a student's proficiency increases, tutors and teachers can point out errors more frequently, but in a way that fosters communication rather than shutting it down.

Learning about culture is an important part of language learning.
Language is a part of culture. To communicate effectively with English speakers, ESL students must often learn both a new language and a new culture. Tutors and teachers play important roles as guides to the new culture, helping students understand the similarities and differences between the culture they encounter in this country and the cultures they bring with them from their native countries. Equipped with this understanding, students will then be able to decide how to blend the two cultures in ways that meet their needs as well as the needs of their families, their employers, and their communities.

Different needs require different solutions.
Because of the diversity among students, ESL teachers and tutors must be prepared to meet the needs of students at different levels, from different cultures, and with a variety of needs and goals. They must be able to assess the students' needs and then select the teaching approaches, techniques, and materials that will meet those needs.

ProLiteracy developed this book as one tool to help ESL teachers and tutors respond to the great diversity of student needs. It is not intended to stand alone but rather to supplement the primary instructional approach or core series being used to teach basic language skills and culture.

ProLiteracy

ProLiteracy, a nonprofit organization based in Syracuse, New York, champions the power of literacy to improve the lives of adults and their families, communities, and societies. It works with adult new readers and learners and with local and national organizations to help adults gain the reading, writing, math, computer, and English language skills they need to be successful. ProLiteracy advocates on behalf of adult learners and the programs that serve them, provides training and professional development, and publishes materials used in adult literacy and basic education instruction. It has 1,100 member programs in all 50 states and the District of Columbia, and it works with 52 nongovernmental organizations in 30 developing countries. ProLiteracy was created in 2002 through the merger of Laubach Literacy International and Literacy Volunteers of America, Inc.

For more information, please visit proliteracy.org.

ProLiteracy
www.proliteracy.org
info@proliteracy.org

New Readers Press
www.newreaderspress.com
nrp@proliteracy.org

Language Learning

The Four Basic Language Skills

One definition of *language* is *a system of symbols that permits people to communicate or interact. These symbols can include vocal and written forms, gestures, and body language.*

The Skills

Another way to describe language is in terms of the four basic language skills: listening, speaking, reading, and writing. In your teaching, you will need to address each of these skills. Whenever possible, you should use activities that integrate all four skills because each reinforces the others.

People generally learn these four skills in the following order:

Listening:	When people are learning a new language (or in the case of children, their first language), they first hear it spoken.
Speaking:	Eventually, they try to repeat what they hear.
Reading:	Later, they see the spoken language depicted symbolically in print.
Writing:	Finally, they reproduce these symbols on paper.

Implications for Teaching

1. Understand that a person first learns to speak by listening. Make sure that students have plenty of opportunity to listen to and understand the spoken language.

2. Set up activities in which students practice speaking by using language they have already heard and understood.

3. Always introduce something new orally (through listening and speaking) before asking students to read it.

4. Always try to create an instructional context that ensures students will understand what they are saying. For example, you might decide to teach the sentence *He is running.* Instead of simply saying it and asking a student to repeat it, you can provide a context by running across the room or showing a picture of someone running. This is especially important with students who are very good at mimicking the sounds of English and who may be able to repeat the words and sentences they hear almost perfectly without understanding anything the speaker is saying.

5. Try to relate the new language to the individual's current language ability as well as his or her previous knowledge and experience. For example, if a student plays a lot of baseball, you can show a picture of a person running to first base to teach the sentence *He is running.* However, such a picture might be inappropriate for a student who has never seen or played baseball.

6. Aim to challenge students appropriately. Although you want to help students understand the material you present, you don't want to make things too easy. The challenge of lesson planning is using material that is appropriate but that also sufficiently challenges students. You can do this by starting with easier activities that provide practice toward a lesson's goal and then gradually using more difficult materials.

The Functions of Language

As you think about how to address each of the four language skills, keep in mind that every time people use language, they do so for a particular purpose or function. Here are some examples:

greeting	parting	inviting	accepting
making excuses	requesting	interrupting	complaining
arguing	complimenting	congratulating	flattering
changing the subject	evading	lying	shifting blame
insulting	criticizing	reprimanding	ridiculing
agreeing	warning	accusing	denying
insisting	disagreeing	apologizing	persuading
reporting	suggesting	reminding	asserting
sympathizing	evaluating	commenting	advising
questioning	commanding	ordering	demanding

Each of these functions has specific language associated with it. To communicate successfully, people need to learn appropriate language to carry out each function. For example, you might teach some of the following phrases if you want to teach about inviting:

Would you like to . . . ?

How would you like to . . . ?

How about . . . ?

I'd be pleased if you would . . .

Another part of language instruction is teaching register—in other words, formal and informal social conventions. The language that students might use with their managers would probably be different from the language they would use with friends.

Second Language Acquisition

In your work as an ESL tutor or teacher, keep in mind that no two students are exactly alike. These are three important areas of difference:

1. Language skill level

    -   Some will speak some English but not be able to read or write it.

    -   Some will be able to read and write English but not speak it.

    -   Some will not be able to read and write in their first language.

    -   Some will have a first language that does not use the Roman alphabet (e.g., Russian, Arabic, or Thai).

    In the Reading and Writing chapter of this book (page 89), you will find a chart that gives further details on the language skill levels as they relate to students' reading and writing abilities. This chart can help guide your teaching techniques.

2. Degree of comfort when trying to speak a new language

    -   Some students are not at all shy about blurting out something in English, and they are not overly concerned about perfect grammar or pronunciation.

    -   Some become embarrassed if they think they are making too many mistakes.

    -   Some think they shouldn't say anything at all unless their English is perfect.

3. Learning rate

    -   Some people can learn a language quickly; others simply don't have a strong knack for picking up languages.

    -   Students who have a lot of contact with English speakers usually progress faster than those who don't.

Keep in mind that it can take several years for adults to become fully proficient in a language. Research with children has found that it takes an average of two to three years to learn conversational skills and five to seven years to master academic language on par with native English speakers, according to the Center for Applied Linguistics' *Education for adult English language learners in the United States: Trends, research, and promising practices* (2010, Washington, D.C.). Those statistics consider the fact that children spend a good portion of their day at school in an English-speaking environment. Consider the implications of this for adults. Because adults are often not immersed in an English-speaking environment all day, language learning can take even longer.

As a result of these differences, no single teaching approach or set of materials can meet the needs of all students—or even all the needs of a single student. As a tutor, you will need to make frequent decisions:

- Which ESL activities and materials should you use?

- How can you motivate students to seek out and communicate with English speakers other than yourself?

- How can you create an effective atmosphere for language learning?

You can make such decisions effectively if you understand the process of second language acquisition—that is, what happens when someone is learning a new language. Inherent in the process of learning a new language are the four principles discussed below.

Principle 1

Meaningful Communication

> Students are more motivated when they are practicing language that has immediate relevance in their lives.

People learning a second language want to learn to say, understand, read, and write things that will be of real and immediate use to them. In the words of one ESL program manager, "Students want something they can learn and use outside of the classroom tomorrow." When they know they can use what they learn, they are more apt to remember it.

As they experience success in using English to communicate in the outside world, students will come to ESL class with more and more self-confidence and enthusiasm: "Hey, I really *am* learning English! I ordered a hamburger today without just pointing to the picture on the menu. I told the waitress what I wanted, and she took my order!"

This is why ESL instruction with adults often focuses on life skills or survival English—that is, learning English to survive in the United States whether at work, at a child's school, on public transportation, at a bank, or in other settings.

IMPLICATIONS FOR TEACHING

1. Use ESL activities and exercises that fulfill a real need for students.

2. Teach students the things *they* want to learn. Find out what their goals are, and teach the skills they need to meet them. You will find more ideas to implement this idea in Chapter 4.

3. Use examples that draw from the students' own lives.

4. Set up role-play activities that model actual situations in which the students will have to use English. This book has suggestions for such activities.

Success, Not Perfection, in the Beginning

> Most ESL students are more concerned about being able to communicate successfully than about being correct.

The important thing for most beginning-level language students is successful communication—not whether the language they use is correct. These students are not focusing on grammar or pronunciation issues but on meeting their basic everyday needs, such as asking directions or mailing a package at the post office. The situation is similar to that of a child who is learning to speak. The child successfully communicates the fact that he or she is thirsty by saying the word *juice*. Neither the child nor the mother is concerned at this stage with the child's inability to correctly say, "May I have a cup of juice, please?"

To begin with, tutors and teachers need to celebrate beginning students' successes rather than focus on their errors. In the story below, an ESL tutor describes his experience with a student from Vietnam.

"Me No Go Work"

A couple of years ago, I was tutoring Canh, a beginning-level ESL student who could barely get by in English. He worked as a custodian at an elementary school. I had been meeting with him twice a week for about three months.

During an ESL lesson on the day after Columbus Day, I asked Canh if he had gone to work the day before. He answered, "Me no go work yesterday."

I was delighted! Canh had used English to answer my question successfully! By his response, I understood that he had not worked yesterday. As his tutor, I wasn't concerned that he said "me" instead of "I." He got the pronoun in the correct place—at the beginning of the sentence.

Not only that, Canh used a negative. He did say "no" instead of "not," but at his stage of English language development, that's OK. He got his idea across!

As students progress from the beginning level to intermediate and advanced levels, error correction becomes more important. Without any error correction, a student's language may become "fossilized"—meaning errors that were not corrected initially become a permanent part of their English repertoire. Tutors must decide when to focus on fluency (fluid communication) and when to focus on accuracy (correct grammar and pronunciation).

IMPLICATIONS FOR TEACHING

1. Be patient and understand that beginning ESL students move from zero ability to near-native fluency in stages clearly marked by a gradual progression from imprecise to accurate levels of English. Rate of progress can be slow, depending on how often a student studies English and is exposed to English outside of tutoring. Allow students to move through each of these stages.

2. Encourage students to communicate in English at every stage, no matter how imprecisely. The very act of communicating is an essential part of the learning process and prepares students to advance to the next stage.

3. Recognize that students need to understand new vocabulary and phrases before they produce them in their own speech. Beginners can understand much more of the new language than they are able to speak. They build from there. This is as true for adults learning a second language as it is for children learning their first language.

4. Focus initially on the skills students require to express what they mean rather than on how the language works (the grammar or rules).

5. Resist the temptation to constantly correct students when they make mistakes. Keep in mind the following points about error correction:

    • Let students know when you really do not understand what they are saying.

    • Correct students when you are trying to teach a specific way of saying something. For example, if you are teaching them to make a request by using the new phrase I *would like . . .* , you will want to make sure they are able to say the phrase correctly.

- Do not correct students during activities such as role plays that are designed to encourage them to concentrate on communicating for meaning. Let them use whatever English they have at their disposal to get their ideas across. You can take notes about any major errors and set aside time afterward to go over corrections.

6. Understand that trying to correct beginners can cause confusion. For example, if I had tried to correct Canh, the results might have been the following:

> **Tutor:** Canh, did you go to work yesterday?
>
> **Canh:** Me no go work yesterday.
>
> **Tutor:** I didn't go to work yesterday.
>
> **Canh:** Oh! You, too, teacher?

Principle 3 *Anxiety*

> Students acquire language more successfully when their anxiety levels are low.

This principle applies to learning anything—not just another language. People seem to be able to learn best when

- they are relaxed.
- they feel comfortable in the class or tutoring environment.
- they know it's OK to make mistakes.
- they are reassured that, overall, they are doing well.

IMPLICATIONS FOR TEACHING

1. Have fun with students, and allow them to have fun, too.

2. Select classroom activities in which students can feel some degree of success. A good example for beginners is Total Physical Response (see Activity 3). It allows students to listen and respond without having to speak.

3. Begin each session with something the students can do well. This might involve playing a short game or practicing vocabulary you have already taught.

4. Don't test students or put them on the spot during the course of conversation or oral activities. Risk is already involved when people are trying out new

language forms, so students' anxiety levels should be kept to a minimum wherever possible during practice activities.

5. Praise! Students feel encouraged when they know they are doing well. Praise students for having the courage to communicate and for mastering material you are teaching.

Exposure

> Progress in a second language depends in part on the amount of exposure students get to speakers of that language.

To move beyond very basic language ability, people must

- have an immediate opportunity to use the language they are studying.

- need to communicate in the new language to get some of their basic needs met.

Some ESL students have little contact with speakers of English apart from their tutors and classmates (if they are in a group setting). Practice might amount to only a few hours per week. As a result, many students reach a plateau, and their progress stops. That's because their most important needs are being met in their first language. They use the first language to discuss topics like family affairs, politics, personal desires, and plans for the future. Such issues are close to them and require complex language for articulating opinions and feelings.

These students may use English only for such basic tasks as asking directions, ordering food, cashing paychecks, or doing jobs that require only a limited number of stock phrases.

IMPLICATIONS FOR TEACHING

1. Devise ways to motivate students to speak about more than superficial things. Talk about current events (as much as you can depending on proficiency levels), and prompt students to talk about their work, families, and lives as much as they are comfortable doing.

2. Encourage and motivate students to have more contact with other speakers of English. At the same time, you can help students identify appropriate contexts for this practice. For example, a student's school-aged children may speak English fluently, but that doesn't necessarily make for the best practice. There is usually a generation gap and a challenge because the adult is an authority figure. It would be more appropriate to practice English with coworkers, neighbors, or others who have a similar hobby or interest.

3. Encourage students to identify specific things they want to be able to say or do that require better English skills. For example, if a student wanted to buy a car, you could

   - teach the student to read the classified ads or help select car ads on the Internet.

   - help the student role-play calls to car owners.

4. Organize role plays and field trips to prepare students to be "out there" on their own with English speakers.

The principles described here are consistent with a communicative approach to teaching ESL—an approach that focuses on enabling people to meet their own needs by using the language to communicate with English speakers.

Becoming a Better Language Teacher

If you are new to teaching in general, to teaching languages, or to teaching adults, the tips below can help make you a more effective teacher:

1. Speak as clearly as you can at a moderate pace. With beginning students, you may have to slow your pace even more.

2. Use simple sentence structures and simple or familiar words. Avoid colloquialisms or idioms (unless they have been explicitly taught in class).

3. Pause frequently to check for comprehension. If a student does not understand, use repetition, rephrasing, or a demonstration, example, or visual.

4. After giving instructions, don't ask, "Do you understand?" Students inevitably answer yes, even when they really don't. Instead, ask students to tell you what they are supposed to do.

5. Encourage students to talk as much as possible.

6. Praise students for their practice.

7. Repeat, repeat, repeat—lesson material, that is. Whenever possible, find ways to incorporate material that you are teaching into subsequent sessions and activities. That repetition is the true key to learning.

8. Work with students on ways to figure out definitions on their own. If a student says "I don't know how to spell that," or "I know what I want to say, but I don't know how to say it," or "I understand most of the sentence, but I don't know this one word," encourage him or her to look at surrounding words for context, look for prefixes or suffixes, consider similar words in the native language, or make inferences/take guesses.

9. Remember that you're teaching adults. It's not the same as teaching language to children. Adults bring a wealth of life experience and, often, work and family experience to the table. Although some material geared toward children may be adapted for adults, you don't want students to feel insulted or talked down to.

10. Connect what you teach to students' lives.

11. Take your time. It is common for new ESL tutors to whiz through material. With experience, you'll find that slowing down and repeating material give students more time to process what they are learning.

12. Be aware of students who "tune out." Observe body language and the degree to which students are participating in the lesson. If students look bored, break into side conversations, or seem to be "tuning out," you may want to speed up the lesson, give a comprehension check, or switch to a different activity. You can also ask students if they would like you to go faster or slower with the material you are presenting.

Communicating Across Cultures

3

By *culture*, we mean the ways and means by which human beings deal with universal human situations and problems using a variety of culture-specific patterns related to values, beliefs, and behaviors in a given social group.

Culture includes all those things that make up our daily lives. It includes social relations, religion, art, beliefs, values, clothes, food, marriage, child rearing, family, education, entertainment, housing, work, and laws.

When people share the same culture, they don't have to spend a lot of time agonizing over what to do or how to act appropriately. Their "cultural maps" help them decide what clothes to wear, what side of the street to drive on, and whether to bow or shake hands when meeting someone.

But ESL students who are new to this country will not have a U.S. cultural map at their disposal. Instead, they constantly have to think about what to do, even in the simplest social situations. Some will just carry out their daily activities according to the same cultural map they have used all their lives—thus running the risk of doing culturally inappropriate things or being misjudged.

As a tutor, you will not only be teaching a new language—you will help the student use that language in a new culture. You will be acting as a guide to the American culture. (Note that the term *American* is used in this section to refer to people who live in the United States or to cultural attitudes and behaviors that are seen as typical of people in this country.)

Language Learning and Culture Learning

The concept of culture, as seen below, represents the various notions of culture. As you can see, learning a new culture is not as simple as just learning the language or social customs. It is actually a complex process involving aspects of culture we can readily observe and aspects that are considered "below the surface." You may not be aware of "below the surface" differences until you become close to someone from a different culture.

The Iceberg Concept of Culture

Like an iceberg, the majority of culture is below the surface.

Surface Culture
Spoken/Conscious Rules
Above sea level
Emotional load: relatively low

food • dress • music
visual arts • drama • crafts
dance • literature • language
celebrations • games

Deep Culture
Unspoken Rules
Partially below sea level
Emotional load: very high

courtesy • contextual conversational patterns • concept of time
personal space • rules of conduct • facial expressions
nonverbal communication • body language • touching
eye contact • patterns of handling emotions
notions of modesty • concept of beauty • courtship practices
relationships to animals • notions of leadership

Unconscious Rules
Completely below sea level
Emotional load: intense

tempo of work • concepts of food • ideals of child rearing
theory of disease • social interaction rate
nature of friendships • tone of voice • attitudes toward elders
concept of cleanliness • notions of adolescence
patterns of group decision making • definition of insanity
preference for competition or cooperation
tolerance of physical pain • concept of "self" • concept of past and future
definition of obscenity • attitudes toward dependents • problem-solving
roles in relation to age, sex, class, occupation, kinship, and so forth

Indiana Department of Education • Office of English Language Learning & Migrant Education • www.doe.in.gov/englishlanguagelearning

Language learning means replacing one language with a new language. A person has little or no freedom to mix and match. Exceptions occur when the person retains words that have no English substitute, such as words for native foods.

On the other hand, *culture learning* is a selective or combining process in which the student decides which elements of the native culture to retain and which elements of the new culture to adapt or adopt. A student's new cultural identity will represent a mixture of the native culture and the new culture. For example, a student may adopt a new way of greeting someone (handshake instead of bow) but maintain the old rule of avoiding eye contact. Students will differ in how much of the new culture they choose to adopt.

Individual Responses to Universal Situations

People of all cultures face the same universal problems or situations, but the cultural responses—the specific ways in which individual cultures handle these situations—can be quite different. The following chart illustrates how this might work for three different universal situations.

CULTURAL ELEMENTS		
Universal	**Culture-Specific**	
	Non-U.S. Culture	**U.S. Culture**
Child rearing	• extended family: everyone (not just the parents) helps out with children (Indonesia, Mexico) • delay in naming newborn child (India)	• nuclear family • child's name often chosen before birth
Food/meals	• chopsticks (China, Japan) • spicy/hot food (India) • third meal very late at night (Spain)	• knife/fork • generally not spicy food • dinner in early evening
Marriage	• formal arrangement; family approval (Middle and Far East)	• personal choice

Not all students will need help with learning U.S. cultural responses. As a tutor, you should simply be alert to areas in which there are likely to be cross-cultural differences.

The following are three examples of possible cultural differences. As you read them, remember that there is no "best" or "only" response to a universal situation. It is often difficult, however, to accept someone else's ways as valid because our own cultural ways are so ingrained in us.

Time

Cultures have different attitudes toward time and punctuality. The American expectation of punctuality differs from expectations in many other countries. For example, a student may consistently drift in late for an ESL session. When this happens, it may be because he or she simply is not accustomed to thinking in terms of exact time. Whether or not you personally have a problem with students who are late to class, you have an obligation to help students understand how others in this country might react to or judge a person who is chronically late.

Here are some specific things that you as a tutor can do in this situation:

- Tell the student that you have only a limited amount of time. The class begins at a certain time and ends at a certain time. If necessary because of the student's limited English ability, use a clock to show starting and ending times. Explain that you must leave when the class ends. Stick to those beginning and ending times for your class sessions.

- If you are teaching a small group or class, tell the students that you always start the session on time to be fair to the other students. Explain that arriving late is disruptive to others who do arrive on time and that people might miss something important if they arrive late.

Attitudes Toward Teachers

Adult students from some cultures may have attitudes toward teachers and tutors that you don't expect. You should be aware of these as you teach. Here are some examples:

- In some cultures, a teacher is revered as a special person—someone who deserves a particularly high level of respect. Students from these backgrounds may balk at addressing a tutor or teacher by his or her first name, even when asked to do so. Be understanding if a student prefers to use *Mr.*, *Mrs.*, or even *Teacher* in addressing you. (The latter is a mark of respect. It is not considered a childish term as it is in the United States.) However, you can still discuss culturally appropriate ways for students to address teachers, employers, and coworkers.

- Although you want to encourage students to think on their own and to be critical in their analysis of new information, students from some cultures may find it difficult to question you or to take risks in the learning situation. In their prior school experiences, such students may have been expected to play a more passive role, simply taking in information without ever initiating any interaction with the tutor or teacher.

- Some students may not want to be seen as the center of attention. In Japan, for example, there is a saying: "The nail that sticks up gets hammered down." Such students may not feel comfortable taking part in role plays.

Encourage, but don't push. (This is more often a problem in small groups and classes than in one-to-one tutoring situations.)

- Asking some students what they want to learn (consistent with the learner-centered approach used in this book) might cause them to question your ability because their expectation is that you will know what you are supposed to teach. In such cases, refer to the needs assessment done when the student entered the program to determine the most appropriate content or teaching methods. When you use teaching techniques that may seem out of the norm to students because of their cultural backgrounds, you can explain your rationale for using them. (For example, a role play can give a student real-world practice using the language.)

- Students from some cultures may be uncomfortable learning in a class with members of the opposite sex because male and female students in their native countries are usually separated after a certain grade in school.

- Some students may feel that teachers who are dressed informally do not take their teaching role seriously.

- Some students may feel uncomfortable disagreeing with your personal opinions and ideas because you are the teacher.

- Some students may have a different view of what language learning should be. For example, they may have learned other languages through textbook grammar exercises instead of the interactive practice often used in adult ESL programs in the United States. They may think the way that English is taught at your program is childish or like a game. You can give such students some of what they consider serious practice and then ask them to participate in the more informal practice that will help them in everyday life.

Eye Contact

In the United States, making eye contact with someone can indicate that you are interested in what they are saying or that you are sincere about what you yourself are saying. A speaker who does not make eye contact can seem shifty or even dishonest. (On the other hand, too much eye contact can be interpreted as staring or being rude.)

But students from some cultures may be reluctant to make eye contact with the tutor or teacher. They have been brought up to believe that it is disrespectful to look a teacher (or other person of authority) in the eye.

Although the amount of eye contact may not cause a problem in the teaching situation itself, you should find a way to discuss it with students. For example, if you are talking about interviewing for a job, you can explain that not looking someone in the eye might be interpreted as a sign of dishonesty in the United States. Or in some cases, it may imply a lack of confidence in one's own abilities. When you create job-related role plays, find a way to help such students practice making eye contact with the (prospective) boss.

Being an Effective Culture Guide

In the role of culture guide, you are helping students discover how American culture "works." Together, you and your students will develop an awareness of each other's cultures—both the similarities and the differences. Enjoy the process!

The tips below may be useful as you think about culture and your role as tutor or teacher and guide.

Tips on Being an Effective Culture Guide

1. **Recognize who you are as a culture guide (examples: age, gender, life experience, personal likes and dislikes).**

    You may be an American, but you also are someone with your own individual cultural roles and experiences. Never pose as the only "real" American. Your own view may be going out of style. By the same token, students do not represent *all* people from their culture. Each person is unique. Avoid stereotyping.

2. **Learn as much about the student's culture as you teach about your own.**

    This helps the student by reinforcing his or her own cultural identity as valid, and it helps you discover points of contrast. An easy way to learn about culture is to ask questions of each other and discuss the answers. "What is a friend in your country?" "What's the best way to find a job in your country?" "What do you like about the United States? What don't you like?" In this way, teacher and student function as mutual culture guides/informants.

3. **Examine similarities as well as differences between the cultures.**

    Similarities bind us together. Differences help us see the many ways we solve universal problems. Both are important. Note the various things your cultures have in common, and explore (respectfully) the ways in which they differ.

4. **Explore cultural meanings found in words, phrases, and gestures.**

    For example, in the United States, there is a difference between referring to someone as "fat" or as "heavyset." The side-to-side head shake is not a universal way to say "no," nor does the "OK" sign with the thumb to forefinger have the same meaning in every culture. Colors, too, carry meanings that can vary across cultures. White is not always for the bride, and black is not always for mourning.

5. **Encourage students to practice guessing what is or is not appropriate in the new culture.**

    Examples: When are gifts expected? What is the right time to arrive for a party? How does one decline an invitation? What do Americans mean when they say, "See you later" or "How's it going?"

6. **Train yourself and the student to be prepared for expressions that are not meant to be taken literally or that have culture-specific meanings.**

   For instance, the expression "Let's get together sometime" does not necessarily mean that the speaker is inviting the listener to a specific engagement. Such invitations are sometimes mere expressions of politeness on a par with the standard "How are you?"

7. **Take time to explore the student's perceptions and conclusions by following up with an observation of your own or a question.**

   When a student describes a situation he or she encounters, you could ask, "What does that mean to you?" or "What did you see going on?" Discussing an event with cultural overtones from the student's life helps bring clarity about cultural issues.

   Sometimes, you may find students making generalizations about American culture (or other cultures that they encounter). Try to refute misinformation in a nonthreatening way. For example, ask, "Why do you think so?" and give the student a chance to explain what is meant. Try offering insights and information that might broaden the student's perspective on the matter, and then tactfully move on to a new topic.

8. **Avoid being judgmental toward yourself or the student.**

   As you build mutual trust, you and the student will realize it's OK to make mistakes in your interpretations of each other's cultural behaviors.

9. **Realize that forming a new identity in a new cultural setting is a matter of personal choice.**

   You can set objectives for what you want to teach about culture. But students must be the ones to decide which parts of the new culture to adapt or adopt. One's cultural identity is a personal work of art.

10. **Be aware that students often experience major adjustment problems.**

    Be supportive, but do not undertake major therapy. Your role is simply to facilitate cultural adjustment as best you can.

(Copyright © 1993 by Louise Damen. Adapted with permission.)

Additional Roles as a Culture Guide

As an ESL tutor, you will often find that you take on other roles with your students. You become a navigator, guiding students through systems and institutions in the United States such as schools, customer service phone trees, courts, and the U.S. government. You help students learn how to be good neighbors and active, responsible members of their communities. These are important aspects of the learning experience, but watch for times when students need help beyond what you can offer. You may find that they actually need a social worker, a lawyer, a doctor, or another professional. In these situations, your program can help you point students toward appropriate resources.

Getting to Know Students

There are two types of ESL student assessment: needs assessment and skills assessment. Together, these create a highly useful multidimensional profile of a student. You will add to this profile as you and a student work together over time. The information you gather from these two assessments will help you to

- identify the student's changing needs, interests, goals, and English abilities.

- make decisions about which skills the student needs to work on and which topics, teaching techniques, and materials are appropriate.

- tailor teaching materials, strategies, and activities to the student's individual needs.

You will find ESL students to be an extremely diverse group. You may tutor a painter from Mexico with a high school education, a former banker from China with a college degree, an engineer from Russia with a Ph.D., or a babysitter from Cameroon with a sixth-grade education. All have very different needs, and the right questions from you can give you insight into their specific learning goals.

For a sample of an initial profile for a new student, see page 165.

Needs Assessment

A needs assessment identifies the student's background, interests, goals, and immediate needs. This knowledge will help you determine what information and skills to teach, as well as what materials and activities to use. A needs assessment is critical to help you make your lessons as student-centered as possible. On the next page are some questions to ask during a needs assessment.

Sample Needs Assessment Inventory

1.	**Name**	I'm your tutor. My name is [Name]. What is your name?
2.	**Homeland**	Where are you from? Tell me about your country.
3.	**Length of time in United States**	How long have you been in the United States?
4.	**Family**	Tell me about your family. What are your children's names? How old are they?
5.	**Job in United States**	What do you do at work? How long have you worked there? What do you like about your job?
6.	**Work experience in homeland**	What kind of work did you do in [Homeland]? For how long? Did you like your work?
7.	**Education**	Did you go to school in [Homeland]? For how many years did you go to school?
8.	**Personal interests**	What do you like to do when you have free time? What did you do last weekend?
9.	**Goals**	What would you like to do in the next five years? Ten years?
10.	**Reasons for learning English**	Why do you want to learn English? Is learning speaking or writing more important to you? (Note: It's fine if the student says both are equally important. You can also ask about the importance of listening skills, reading, grammar, and pronunciation for them.) What do you want to be able to do that you can't do now? How will learning English help you reach your goals?

Don't expect to complete the needs assessment inventory in one meeting. Many of the questions will be answered as you get to know the student better.

Goal setting is an ideal way to guide lesson activities and give purpose to them. The following activity can help you set goals with students.

(Note: All activities in this book are marked with a designation of appropriate level—beginning, intermediate, advanced, or all.)

Setting Goals (all)

PURPOSE

To help students set and reach their goals.

POSSIBLE GOALS

Work	Family and Home
Fill out a job application	Help my children in school
Write a résumé	Read a book in English to my children
Speak English in a job interview	Make a family budget
Write a report	Save money for a family vacation
Find a new job	Buy a house
Ask my manager for a raise	Plan healthy meals for my family

Self	Community
Fill out forms	Vote in a local election
Open an email account	Read local street signs and names
Become a citizen	Participate in my local civic organization
Get my driver's license	Get and use a library card
Learn how to type	Volunteer at my local homeless shelter
Get my GED	Learn the history of my community

METHOD

1. When you have a new student, use the Goals Worksheet on the next page. Depending on a student's proficiency level, you may need to help him or her consider exact goals. The boxed list of possible goals above may provide some ideas. Encourage students to include goals that go beyond what you will cover in your sessions. Academic goals could fall under "Self" or even one of the other categories. Explain to students that setting specific goals will make it possible for you to teach material relevant to their needs.

Goals Worksheet

Family and Home

_____

_____

_____

_____

Work

_____

_____

_____

_____

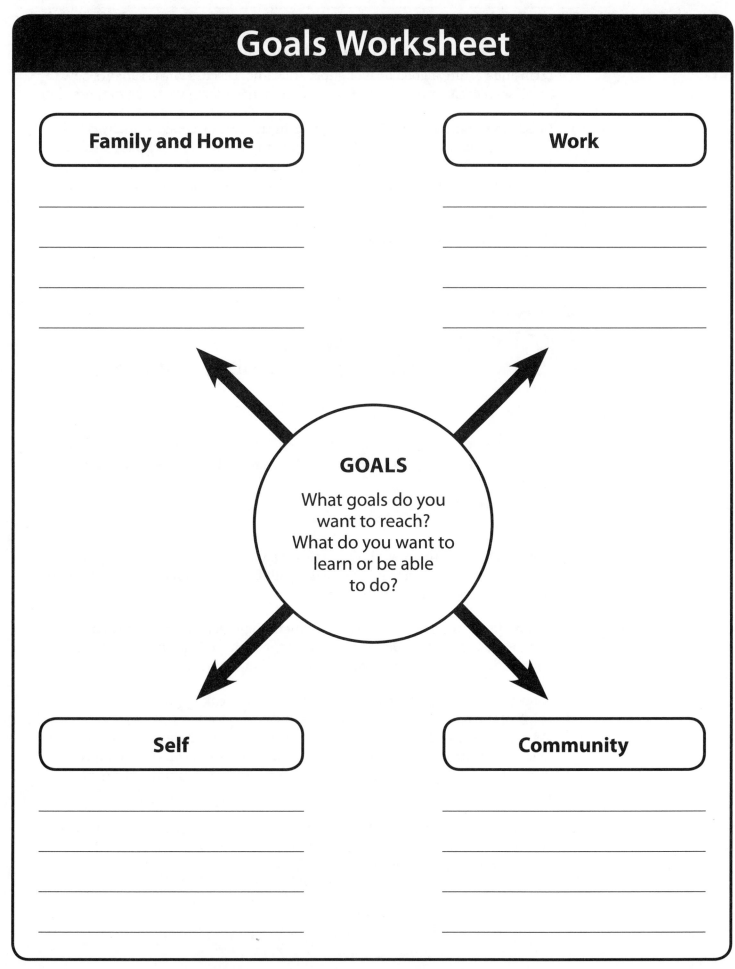

GOALS

What goals do you
want to reach?
What do you want to
learn or be able
to do?

Self

_____

_____

_____

_____

Community

_____

_____

_____

_____

2. Break goals into manageable steps. You will likely find that some goals are long term and require a good deal of effort and time. Discuss with students how to break such goals into manageable steps. Then have them write down those steps.

3. Check on progress. As students progress in their lessons, occasionally check on their goals and discuss progress. For example, a student who is learning English to help a child in school might note when she learns to read a report card. Then she might want to set a goal of participating in a parent-teacher conference.

(Adapted from "Getting Students to Their Goals." Notebook, Winter 2011, pp. 8–10.)

Activity 2

The Language Wheel
(high-beginning, intermediate, or advanced)

PURPOSE

To help students develop the oral skills they need in specific situations in their everyday lives. (This is a good activity to help students link an ESL session to the outside world.)

METHOD

1. Ask each student to draw a large circle on paper and write his or her name in the middle of it. Model this by drawing your own circle on a piece of paper and writing your own name in the middle.

2. Ask students to think of some places where they speak English in their daily lives. Have them list these places around the inside of the circle. Model this yourself in your own circle. See the example on the next page.

3. After they have listed several places where they speak English, tell students to think of the person or people with whom they typically speak in those places. Tell them to draw lines outward from the edge of the circle at the name of each place. Then ask them to write the names of these people on the appropriate lines. Model this for them on your own circle. See the example on the next page.

4. When they finish, have students briefly describe their wheels to you. Explain that the wheel is a useful visual way to identify where they most need to strengthen their English skills.

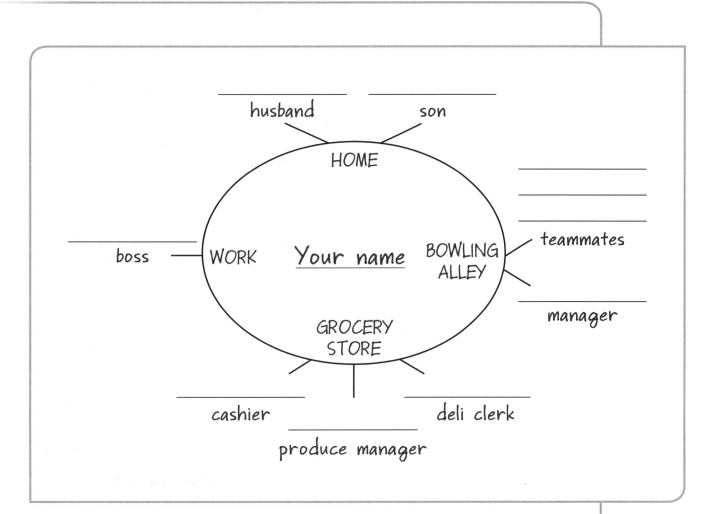

Skills Assessment

A skills assessment reveals a student's current English language listening, speaking, reading, and writing abilities. Skills assessments may be done at three different points:

1. To find out what a student's skills are upon entering a program (part of the intake process)

2. To measure a student's progress periodically during learning

3. To measure progress and to determine appropriate referrals for additional assistance when a student leaves a program

ESL programs use many different methods to assess students' skills. (For references to a few commonly used assessment tools, see Appendix B.) You can also do your own informal assessment, such as the following example for a beginning student:

Sample Skills Assessment

Comprehension
Does the student understand anything at all that you say?

Does the student understand simple commands or directions?

Does the student ask you—or gesture for you—to repeat?

Speaking
Is the student's speech intelligible, or do you have to keep asking him or her to repeat?

Is the student's speech fluent, that is, can he or she maintain a flow of understandable speech, whether or not it is grammatically accurate?

Does the student pronounce individual sounds reasonably well?

Is the student's intonation pattern at all close to that of American English?

Does the student speak with any degree of grammatical accuracy?

Reading
Can the student read his or her name?

Can the student read simple signs?

Writing
Can the student hold a pen or pencil properly?

Can the student print or write his or her own name using the Roman (English) alphabet?

Can the student fill in blanks on a form?

The activities described below will help you get this information.

"HELLO, HOW ARE YOU?"

When you meet a student for the first time, use a basic everyday greeting such as "Hello, how are you?" If the student says nothing and has a blank look, it probably means that he or she is not able to understand the greeting. Since basic greetings are always introduced in beginning-level ESL classes, you could assume that overall the student understands very little oral English.

If the student responds with something like "Fine, thank you," note the accuracy of his or her pronunciation. Is it close to native English pronunciation? Does he or she have good pronunciation of individual sounds but not the appropriate intonation pattern?

If the student responds with something like "Me good," he or she is probably at the beginning level with some exposure to English.

TEACHING ADULTS: AN ESL RESOURCE BOOK

"MY NAME IS _____. WHAT'S YOUR NAME?"

Asking this question will give you additional information about the student's skills. Does the student make some attempt to provide his or her name?

"READ YOUR NAME."

Have two name tags ready, one with your name printed on it and one with the student's name. Point to your name tag and say, "My name is _____." Hand the other name tag to the student. Point to it and ask, "Please read." If he or she looks confused, point again and draw your finger along the name. Give the student time to respond.

"WRITE YOUR NAME."

Ask the student to write his or her name. If necessary, point to your own name tag. Say, "My name is _____." Print your name on a piece of paper as you repeat, "My name is _____." Then ask the student to do the same. Keep in mind that the student might be able to write his or her name but not be able to understand your request.

"FOLLOW THE DIRECTIONS."

Be prepared with a series of tasks that require only physical (not oral) responses. Examples: "Please give me the _____." "Come with me." "Please sit here." Note how well the student is able to carry out the requests. A related idea is to ask the student to identify colors or articles of clothing that someone is wearing.

"TALK ABOUT THE PICTURE."

Ask the student a series of questions about a picture you bring to class. Start with easy questions. Then go on to more difficult ones.

"TELL ME ABOUT _____ IN YOUR COUNTRY."

If you suspect that a student is at an intermediate or advanced level of English, try to engage him or her in a light conversation about home. You might ask him to talk about the differences between food, shopping, or music in his country and in the United States. Listen for her ability to give two or three concrete examples. Generally speaking, the more detail a student is able to give in language that you can understand easily, the higher his or her language level.

Keep the following tips in mind when you assess skills:

- Give the student time to respond. Silence does not mean that nothing is happening. The student may need time to think.

- Remember that most students understand more than they can say. This is a normal stage of development, so don't assume that the student has some unusual problem with his or her speaking skills. (The same applies to students who seem to read better than they can write.)

Learning Styles and Multiple Intelligences

It can be helpful to know a student's preferred learning style so you can present activities in a way that helps him or her comprehend them more easily. A person's learning style can be visual, auditory, or kinesthetic. Some people combine styles. A visual learner comprehends information best by seeing it in written or graphic form. An auditory learner understands information best by hearing it. A kinesthetic learner learns best by doing something.

If you know a student's learning style, you can present information in the way the student learns best—not just in your personally preferred learning style.

If you are teaching students at an intermediate or advanced level, you can ask them simple questions to help identify their preferred learning styles. You can even have them take a simple learning style assessment. You can find tests online by using the search terms "learning style questionnaire" and "learning style assessment."

Here are a few tips to better accommodate each learning style.

Visual learners often respond best to these techniques:

- Using flashcards
- Using a highlighter to highlight important information
- Clearing the work space of distracting objects
- Using diagrams and charts

Auditory learners often respond best to the following:

- Thinking aloud
- Playing music in the background to enhance learning
- Listening to instructions orally as well as seeing them on paper
- Listening to and telling stories

Kinesthetic learners often respond best to these activities:

- Teaching with objects

- Doing role plays

- Making physical movements that reinforce learning

- Taking breaks when they can move around

You may also have heard about multiple intelligences. This line of thought, proposed by Howard Gardner in 1983, suggests that we all have stronger abilities in certain areas of learning: visual-spatial, bodily-kinesthetic, musical, interpersonal, intrapersonal, linguistic, logical-mathematical, and naturalistic. This information is not specific to ESL instruction. However, knowing the area(s) in which your students are strongest can help you identify the best way to present class material. It can also help you find opportunities for students to share their talents; for example, if a student has strong musical ability, he or she may want to demonstrate that at some point. You can find assessments online for multiple intelligences by using the search term "multiple intelligences quiz." These tests may not be written in language simple enough for beginning students, but you could possibly use them with higher-level students or for your own personal assessment.

Listening and Speaking

When you tutor beginning-level ESL students, always start with the oral language skills of listening and speaking. These will most quickly and directly aid beginning students in their daily lives.

The activities in this section are intended for use with beginning-level students, but you can easily adapt them for students at all levels. More advanced students also need to work on their oral skills to improve their ability to understand spoken English and produce English conversation. Advanced students may need listening and speaking practice in areas such as these: expressing abstract ideas, following social language conventions, using informal versus formal language, participating in academic or work discussions, making academic or work presentations, recognizing implied meanings, understanding broadcast/news speech, and using technical language.

Guidelines for Teaching Oral Skills

You may find these guidelines useful when you teach oral skills:

1. Don't worry about not being able to communicate—even when students don't know a word of English. There are effective strategies for teaching English to beginners even when you do not speak their language. For example, Total Physical Response, described on pages 43–46, is an ideal teaching technique to use with students who are at this basic level.

2. Use gestures to indicate when students should listen, speak, or stop speaking. These gestures are especially important when you work with beginning-level students and will make initial lessons go much more smoothly. In time, students will understand what to do. Then you will only need to use gestures when introducing a new drill or exercise.

3. Whisper the student's lines to help him or her get started. Mouthing or whispering establishes that the line is the student's line, not yours. For example, when you are practicing a dialogue, a student may not be able to

TEACHING ADULTS: AN ESL RESOURCE BOOK

remember the next line. In this case, simply begin to mouth or whisper it, and use the beckon gesture to encourage the student to repeat it aloud.

4. Focus on teaching the words, phrases, and grammatical structures that students must know to meet everyday needs. Examples of relevant situations might be applying for a job, renting an apartment, or buying groceries. Your goal is to enable students to take what was just learned in the tutorial and use it immediately in the outside world.

5. Use objects or pictures—often called *realia* in ESL teaching terminology—to illustrate the meanings of words or to help students understand the context of an activity. For example, when doing a role play about making a bank deposit, you could use blank counter checks and deposit slips, personal identification, and a picture of the inside of a bank.

Select pictures to meet your teaching needs. For example, pictures of single objects can be used to teach vocabulary or grammar. Pictures showing a sequence can be used to demonstrate steps in a process, such as changing a tire or tying a necktie. Pictures that have a lot of elements and action have a wide variety of applications. You can ask students to describe what is happening in such pictures or to imagine what the people in the picture are thinking.

A good picture dictionary designed for ESL students can suffice for many of the picture-related needs you might have. However, you may also find it helpful as a tutor to develop your own picture file. Magazines, newspapers, and the Internet are excellent sources. To make the file most useful, divide the pictures into categories. Here are a few examples:

animals

clothing

foods (This category can be broken down into smaller categories such as fruits, vegetables, desserts.)

occupations

opposites (*big/small, tall/short, happy/sad*)

sports

unusual things (great as conversation starters)

grammar or structures (Pictures can be used to teach things like action verbs, such as *running*.)

Search engines on the Internet can provide a multitude of images from which you can select. Just type in the name of the concept you would like to show, and the search engine will likely come up with a variety of results. Online searches are also helpful if you are in a tutoring session and have access to the Internet via a computer or smartphone. For example, if you are teaching a word and you are not sure how to draw it or students have trouble understanding it, you can look for images of that word online.

6. Do not assume that students don't understand a word or phrase just because they are unable to say it or are reluctant to try. Even beginning students are usually able to understand more than they can say themselves. However, they need to start speaking as much as possible if they wish to improve. You can encourage nonverbal responses like pointing, acting something out, or answering yes-or-no questions to check for comprehension.

7. Remember that students will make lots of errors as they are learning to speak English. This is a natural part of the learning process. It doesn't mean that they are not making progress or that you are doing a poor job of teaching.

8. Make corrections only at appropriate times. For example, it would not be appropriate to interrupt spontaneous practice in a role play to correct for grammar or pronunciation. This is a time when the student's goal is to express ideas, not to speak with perfection. Set aside a time after activities such as role plays to suggest ways that students might phrase or pronounce things more effectively in the future.

9. Be patient. Give students plenty of time to respond to your questions or requests. Learn to be comfortable with silence while students are thinking about what to say or how to say it.

Introducing New Vocabulary

The first step in teaching oral skills is to help students acquire a basic vocabulary of useful words and phrases. It can take as many as 20 or more exposures to a new word in written or oral form for a language learner to truly understand that word. Keep in mind the following guidelines when you are teaching vocabulary:

1. Teach only a few new words at a time. Aim for no more than 8 to 10 new words per lesson.

2. With a beginning-level student, choose one way of saying something and stick with it. For example, if you teach the expression "Turn off the light," don't give other versions of the same expression ("Switch off the light," "Turn out the light," or "Put out the light").

3. Teach vocabulary in a consistent fashion. Aim for a routine each time you introduce a new group of words. For example, you might routinely follow these steps:

   a. Say each word and have students listen while they look at the words on a page from a book or handout.

   b. Have students listen as you say each word again, and then ask them to repeat it. At this time, discuss the meanings of the words.

   c. Have students practice each word again at their own pace.

That said, you can vary your routine from time to time depending on the words you are teaching. Some vocabulary lessons work better with hands-on practice during presentation.

4. Use repetition. To learn new words permanently, students need to hear and use them over and over again. Your teaching routine should include recycling new words in later lessons. Here's an example:

   > You are helping a student prepare for a job interview, and you are teaching related vocabulary words such as *application, manager, interview,* and *thank-you note.* You present the vocabulary, practice it in a comprehension exercise, and have the student use the vocabulary in sentences. In the next class, you can review the words through a game, a dictation, or a job interview role play.

5. Help to teach a new word by showing several examples of the object or picture. That way, there is no danger that students will misunderstand what the word means. For example, to teach the word *pencil,* show students three different types of pencils. If you use only one, students might think that you are teaching the word *yellow, straight,* or *write.*

6. Encourage students to record new words with the help of digital recorders or smartphones. A digital recorder is inexpensive and can be a valuable tool for a language learner.

7. Ask students to create personal dictionaries where they enter new words as they learn them. At the top of each page, have them write one letter of the alphabet. (A loose-leaf binder makes it easy to add pages if that becomes necessary.) When a new word is introduced, they can write it and a definition on the appropriate page. Some students may want to add a translation of the word into their language. An example sentence using the word or a small picture illustrating it could be added as well.

Total Physical Response (TPR)

Total Physical Response (TPR) is a teaching technique that enables students to learn new vocabulary by listening to and carrying out spoken commands. In TPR activities, students are not required to speak. The tutor models the commands and continually repeats and reviews them until the students can carry out the commands with no difficulty. Students are more likely to be and feel successful when the tutor provides constant support and modeling and eliminates the pressure on them to speak the new words.

TPR is most useful with those who understand little or no English.

With beginning students, first teach basic commands that call for simple body movements and no props: *stand up, sit down, walk,* and *turn around.* This gives them a welcome feeling of accomplishment and helps them become comfortable with TPR right away.

Students can go on to more advanced TPR activities in which they interact with props and people in the learning environment. Examples of commands to use at this stage are *touch the, point to, pick up, put down,* and *give me.*

You can also use TPR for the following purposes:

- To review and reinforce vocabulary you have already taught using non-TPR methods

- To use as a "catch-up" at the beginning of a lesson for the benefit of students who have missed previous lessons in which new material was introduced (This is obviously more appropriate for a small group or class versus a one-to-one context.)

- To provide students with an enjoyable, relaxing break during a lesson

All TPR activities include the four basic steps shown below.

Activity 3 — *Basic Steps for* TPR (beginning)

PURPOSE

To teach new vocabulary in a way that allows students to show they understand without requiring them to produce new words from memory.

METHOD

1. Select five to seven new commands (and any related vocabulary) to teach.

2. Before the teaching session, make a list of all the commands in the order you plan to teach them. (The list will serve as a record of what you have taught and will help you plan review activities for later lessons.)

3. Gather any equipment, props, or pictures you will need to set the context or illustrate the meaning of the commands. For example, if you are teaching *stand up, sit down, pick it up,* and *put it down,* you would list those commands and make sure you have a chair and a couple of pencils or books to use for demonstration.

   If you will be teaching commands that involve objects, bring to the lesson two examples of each object. This will allow you to model the command using one object and to have the student use the other object to carry out the command at the same time.

4. If you are working with a group, select two or three students for the demonstration.

(Teaching more than one student at the same time takes the pressure off any individual student. The other students in the class will also be learning as they watch. When you finish the demonstration, you can invite others to carry out the commands they saw you teach.)

5. Teach the commands.

    a. Model the action as you give the first command. Speak slowly and clearly. As you do this, try using gestures and facial expressions to help students understand what you want them to do.

    b. Perform the action with the student several times, and give the command each time.

    c. Give the command without performing the action yourself. Encourage the student to indicate comprehension by performing the action.

    d. If the student has difficulty carrying out the command, model the action again as you say it. Always be ready to help out if necessary.

    e. Repeat steps a–d for each command you plan to teach. Before introducing each new command, review the commands you have already taught. Review them in the same order that you taught them.

    f. Finally, review all the commands in random order.

    g. If you are working with a small group, have selected students practice giving the commands.

SUGGESTIONS

- Go slowly. If you go too fast, students are likely to become confused and tense and make mistakes. They will learn best if they are relaxed and feel comfortable with the activity. TPR should always be light and fun.

- Provide whatever support the students need to be successful. If students are not successful in carrying out a command, you have gone too fast, included too much material, or asked them to do something you did not adequately teach and model.

- Use TPR lessons to practice real-life activities. Examples: baking a cake, addressing an envelope, getting dressed to go out in winter, washing one's hands, setting the table, or routines for waking up and going to work or to class.

You will find a variety of resources that describe more TPR techniques online. One such resource is *TPR: A Curriculum for Adults* by Margaret Silver, Barbara Adelman, and Elisabeth Price of the English Language and Literacy Center, St. Louis, MO (2003). It is available at **http://www.springinstitute.org/Files/tpr4.pdf**.

Foam Balls (beginning)

PURPOSE

To introduce speaking using TPR. (This activity is appropriate with a small group or in a classroom setting.)

METHOD

1. Throw a soft foam ball to Student A, saying, "[Name], catch the ball." When Student A catches the ball, say, "[Name], throw the ball to me." Use appropriate gestures to convey your meaning.

2. Throw the ball to Student B, saying, "[Name], catch the ball."

3. Ask, "Who has the ball?" Model the answer: "[Name] has the ball."

4. Call on two or three students by name, and gesture for them to repeat this response. (Model again if necessary.)

5. Tell Student B, "[Name], throw the ball to [name of Student C]."
    (If necessary, use gestures to convey your meaning. Point to Student B and make a throwing gesture in the direction of Student C.)

6. Make a beckoning gesture with your hand (and mouth the statement if necessary) to encourage Student B to say to Student C, "[Name], catch the ball."

7. Call on other students and ask, "Who has the ball?" Model the appropriate answer as needed.

8. Ask students to continue to throw the ball to each other while they say, "[Name], catch the ball." Each time the ball is caught, you will ask two or three students, "Who has the ball?"

9. Provide help as needed, modeling correct responses and encouraging the students to speak—not just throw and catch.

Vocabulary Drills

You can also use vocabulary drills to teach new vocabulary. Unlike TPR activities, vocabulary drills always require students to give an oral response. These drills can also enable students to interact with each other as they handle or point to objects or as they talk about the objects using their new vocabulary.

Here are some general principles for doing vocabulary drills:

1. Even if students can already read English, help them to acquire new vocabulary orally first. After they have heard and practiced new words orally several times, you can write the new words to show them the written form.

2. Take the time to explain any new words that come up during the activity but that you had not planned to teach.

3. Encourage questions, and don't worry if unexpected conversations take place.

4. When teaching vocabulary or grammatical structures, make sure that students always say what is true for them. For example, you might point to one student's book. Say, "This is *my* book." When the student repeats the statement, it will be true for him or her. If you said, "This is *your* book," the statement would not be true when the student repeated it.

Activity 5
Vocabulary Drill to Teach Direction Words
(beginning)

PURPOSE

To teach the English directional words *left, right, above, below*.

METHOD

1. Choose several objects whose names the students already know. The following example uses tools: a hammer, a screwdriver, a wrench, and a pair of pliers. (If you don't want to practice tools, you could use more generic office/school objects, such as a pen, a cup, a pencil, a piece of paper, and a book.)

2. Arrange the tools on the table. Review the names of the tools with the students, using the question "What's this?" Reteach the words if the students are not sure of them.

3. Sit down next to (not across from) a student. (Sitting across from the student can cause confusion: "Whose left? Yours or mine?")

4. Place a piece of paper (or a magazine or similar object) on the table.

5. Teach: *left*
        right

    a. Place the hammer to the left of the piece of paper and say, "The hammer is on the left."

b. Repeat the statement and beckon for the student to say it after you.

c. Move the hammer to the right of the piece of paper. Say, "The hammer is on the right." Gesture for the student to repeat the statement after you.

d. Gesture for the student to be silent. Then say, "Where's the hammer? The hammer is on the right." Repeat both the question and the answer.

e. Ask the question again: "Where's the hammer?" Encourage the student to respond. Help if necessary.

f. Move the hammer back to the left of the piece of paper, and ask the student, "Where's the hammer?" Beckon the student to respond.

g. Repeat step 5 using another tool.

6. Teach: *above*
below

a. Hold the hammer above the table and say, "The hammer is above the table."

b. Ask the student, "Where's the hammer?" If he or she is unable to respond correctly, model the correct answer again, and beckon the student to repeat it.

c. Put the hammer below the table and say, "The hammer is below the table." Ask the student, "Where's the hammer?" Model the answer again if he or she has difficulty responding.

7. As students learn more, have them place the tools themselves and ask each other where the tools are. The steps above are just an introduction to direction words.

SUGGESTION

You can use these same steps to introduce other direction words and prepositions such as *next to, on top of,* or *in front of.*

Reinforcing Vocabulary

It's important to provide plenty of opportunities for students to review any new vocabulary. Only through repeated use will they come to "own" it and be able to use it outside of class. Follow-up games, role plays, and simulations of real-world situations all help students internalize new vocabulary and connect it to their daily lives.

The follow-up activity on the next page is designed to reinforce new vocabulary. Various other activities throughout this book are also appropriate to help students make new vocabulary their own.

Activity 6

Eating Utensils (all)

PURPOSE

To help students review vocabulary related to eating utensils, directional words, prepositions, and commands. (This activity is particularly useful with beginning-level students. Note that this activity is for a small-group setting, not one-to-one tutoring.)

METHOD

1. Review the vocabulary that will be used: *pick up, put, left, right, on top of, in front of, under, above, cup, bowl, plate, knife, fork,* and so on. (You will have previously taught this vocabulary.)

2. Demonstrate the activity below with a student as the others watch. You will give the instructions. The student will follow them.

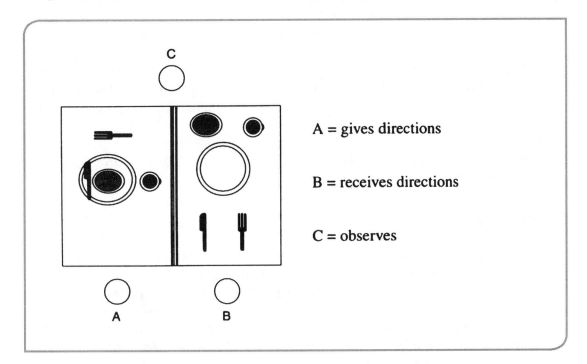

A = gives directions

B = receives directions

C = observes

3. After you finish the demonstration, place students in groups of three. Two of the students in each group (Students A and B) sit next to each other on one side of a table. The third student (Student C) sits across the table facing them. During the activity, each student will take a turn at each role: giver of instructions, receiver of instructions, and observer.

4. Give one set of eating utensils (cup, bowl, plate, knife, and fork) to Student A and an identical set to Student B.

5. Give each group a folded cardboard "tent" to use as a table divider.

6. Have Student B face away from the table. Tell Student C to arrange the eating utensils (in any configuration) in front of Student A.

7. Place the cardboard divider on the table between Student A and Student B so that Student B cannot see Student A's utensils. (Student A will need to see Student B's utensils, however, to give Student B any needed direction during the activity.)

8. When the divider is in place, tell Student B to turn around to face the table but not to look at Student A's utensils.

9. Ask Student A to tell Student B how to arrange the utensils so that they match Student A's arrangement. Student A can use only English and should not use gestures. ("Pick up the cup and put it on top of the plate." "Put the fork to the left of the bowl.") Student A should watch what Student B does and make verbal corrections where necessary. ("No, to the *left* of the bowl, not the right. Yes, that's it.")

10. When students are doing this activity for the first time, don't increase the pressure by setting a time limit. Let everyone try to complete the task. Offer help or encourage the observers to do so if anyone has problems.

11. When Student A completes the task, have the students in each group change roles and repeat the task. Then have them change roles again and repeat the task once more. In this way, each person has an opportunity to play all three roles.

12. The next time you use this activity, you can set a three-minute time limit to add to the challenge.

SUGGESTIONS

- In a one-to-one teaching situation, try alternating the roles of giver and receiver of instructions with the student. Since there will be no observer, the person giving the instructions also takes on the observer's tasks.

- Consider doing the same activity using real objects from the classroom, house, or workplace for additional real-world practice. If you do this, be sure that the students already know the names of the objects.

- Use pictures in place of real objects.

- Have a competition among the groups to see who can complete the task in the shortest amount of time. In this case, Student C becomes the timekeeper.

Activity 7

Focused Listening/Listening to a Story (all)

PURPOSE

To practice listening comprehension and speaking skills in the context of a story.

METHOD

1. Use a story that you would like to introduce to your students. Tell the students that you will complete a listening exercise related to the story.

2. Share the title of the story with the students and any pictures that are part of the story. Ask the students to predict what the story will be about.

3. Identify any vocabulary from the story that might be unfamiliar, and pre-teach it.

4. Tell the students to listen carefully while you read the story. Ask them to listen for the general idea of the story—details will come later. Without showing the text, read the story aloud at a moderate to slow pace.

5. Ask a student to retell the story. Ask: "What do you remember?"

6. Read the story aloud a second time. This time, pause occasionally in your reading to ask comprehension questions.

(Activity courtesy of Lynne Weintraub.)

SUGGESTIONS

- There are a number of websites where students can listen to audio files to practice focused listening. You can broaden their focused listening tasks to include discussions and summaries. The following page on the ITESL *Journal* site is a good reference: **http://iteslj.org/links/ESL/Listening/Podcasts**.

- New Readers Press has a number of resources that are also good for focused listening, such as *That's Life* and *Life Goes On*. The stories are short, are geared toward adults, use simple vocabulary, and are relevant to everyday contexts.

- Another New Readers Press resource is *News for You*. This easy-to-read news publication provides seven news stories each week and is available both in print and online. In the online version, audio for each story is appropriate for focused listening. See **http://newreaderspress.com** for more information.

Dictation for Listening Skills (all)

PURPOSE

To help students hone their listening skills through dictation.

METHOD

1. Choose a written passage with vocabulary that the student has already studied. This could be words, sentences that you have written, or sentences from a text. The lower the student's level, the fewer words you'll want to use in your practice.

2. Read the passage to the student. Repeat each word or phrase two times. Ask the student to write what he or she hears.

3. Have the student show you what he or she has written so you can check the answers.

SUGGESTIONS

*   If you are teaching a small group or class, you can have students dictate words or sentences to each other once they understand how dictation works (this will work more smoothly in high-beginning, intermediate, and advanced classes).

*   Another idea for a small group or class is to have students take turns writing their answers on the board. They can check what's on the board for accuracy.

Idioms

An idiom is a group of words that means something different from what the individual words might suggest. Intermediate and advanced students need to understand idioms to become fully proficient. Idioms can be two- or three-word verbs, such as

*   *call off* (cancel).

*   *get across* (convey an idea).

*   *think up* (invent).

*   *read up on* (get information about).

*   *cut down on* (lessen).

Idioms can also be expressions, such as

- *in the long run.*

- *push over the edge.*

- *through thick and thin.*

The difficulty with idioms is that although students might already know the meanings of the individual words in the idiom, this will not help them decipher the meaning of the idiom as a whole.

As a tutor, you should teach common English idioms that students need to know. But you should also be aware of your own use of idioms in the classroom. If students look confused, it may be because you just used an idiom that sounds strange in its literal translation. Try to be aware of your use of idioms, and if you work with a beginner, screen all but the most common idioms out of your speech. With an intermediate- or advanced-level student, check to be sure that the student understands your meaning, and if necessary, follow up with an alternate way of phrasing your sentence that does not use the idiom.

The key to teaching an idiom is to put it in context—that is, to create a story or scenario that illustrates the idiom so the student will understand it and recognize it outside of class. A recorded conversation is a useful way to present such a story or scenario. Keep in mind that you can teach more than one idiom at a time.

Activity 9

Writing a Conversation to Teach Idioms
(intermediate, advanced)

PURPOSE

To teach the meaning of idioms by using them in a conversational context.

METHOD

1. Select the idioms you want to teach, and explain them (examples: *all set, call off, take an exam, change his mind, read up on, push over the edge, in the long run*). The idioms you choose might come from a reading passage you are planning to use. Aim for no more than about eight idioms at a time. Explaining idioms becomes even easier if you have visuals that can explain their meaning. Go over the meanings, see if students have any questions, and have them practice pronunciation.

2. Have the students practice using the idioms in sentences.

3. After you have practiced the idioms a few times and feel confident that the students understand them (this may happen after one or two class periods),

work with them to write a conversation between two people that incorporates these idioms.

Example:

> **Maria:** Hey, Fred, are things all set for Mike's birthday party?
>
> **Fred:** I'm sorry, Maria, but we have to call off the party.
>
> **Maria:** Oh, no! Why?
>
> **Fred:** Mike has to take a history exam the next day.
>
> **Maria:** You can't get him to change his mind and come to the party anyway?
>
> **Fred:** I tried, but he'll just be too busy reading up on his American history.
>
> **Maria:** I guess I understand. Final exams are enough to push anyone over the edge.
>
> **Fred:** We could change the date. In the long run, that might be best. Mike will really be ready for a party after the exam!

4. Go through the conversation. Help students correct grammar, spelling, or usage errors.

5. Practice the conversation aloud with the students. If they are more advanced, you can discuss ways to lengthen the conversation.

SUGGESTIONS

- There are idiom textbooks and idiom dictionaries geared toward ESL students. If idioms are a focus in your lessons, you may want to use one of these resources or to refer your students to them.

- Caution students to use idioms with care. Understanding them is wonderful, but it can be more challenging to use them correctly. One program coordinator had a student who said, "Leave a message and I'll get back *at* you"!

- When discussing idioms or new vocabulary, your student may ask you about slang, physiological terms they've heard (e.g., *vomit*, *nausea*), and perhaps profanity. You can help explain this language but also point out which of these words or phrases are inappropriate in most social settings.

Grammar

Grammar is the structure of a language. It is the set of rules specifying the ways words are inflected (how endings are added to change the meaning) and the ways individual words can be combined into larger units to form phrases, clauses, or sentences. Learning individual vocabulary words is helpful, but an ESL student will have difficulty communicating without also understanding English grammatical structures.

During your lessons, you will be trying to replicate actual situations in the outside world in which students have to use English to get their needs met. When possible, you should try to incorporate grammar instruction into these real-life contexts rather than present it in isolation. In this way, students will be better able to actually use the grammar when they need it. However, as students become more advanced, they will want and need more explicit grammar instruction. There are a number of grammar textbooks in adult ESL that you can use when your students become more proficient.

An example of teaching grammar in isolation might be the following: You are working with a student who already knows the word *sit*, and you want to teach the past tense *sat*. You could do the following:

- Say, "I sit in the chair" while you do the action.

- Stay seated and say, "I sat in the chair."

- Have the student repeat each of these sentences.

- Have the student practice saying pairs of sentences using other familiar verbs:
    I eat dinner. I ate dinner.
    I play with my son. I played with my son.

Students can and do learn this way. However, they seem to learn much better when they are involved in activities that give them a chance to use grammar in a context that is relevant to real life. Many ESL texts contain activities that teach grammar in context, so you will not have to create all of these activities yourself. Examples of such "in-context" activities include the following:

- Use recipes to teach count and noncount nouns (e.g., words such as *egg* where you can count how many items there are [12 eggs] and words such as *milk* that you cannot actually count).

- Play a game of catch using TPR to teach the following:

    Pronouns as direct objects: *"Throw the ball to [Name]."*
                                    "Throw it to [Name]."

    Pronouns as objects of prepositions: *"Throw the ball to Anna."*
                                            "Throw the ball to her."

- Ask questions where students need to use the correct tense of verbs they have recently learned. For example, you can say, "What do you do every day?" "What did you do yesterday?" "What will you do tomorrow?" "What did you eat?" "Where did you go?" "What did you wear?"

If a student is having difficulty mastering a specific grammatical form, you can stop the activity and spend a few minutes doing a repetitive drill such as the one described below in Activity 10. After completing the drill, return to the original activity, and give the student another chance to use the new grammatical form in context.

The Internet has a wealth of resources to help adult ESL students practice grammar. Some of these resources involve online practice, while others are handouts you can print and use without Internet access:

- For computer-based practice with beginning students, you can try the following link on the website Manythings.org: **http://www.manythings.org/e/grammar.html**.

- You can find a variety of printable handouts organized by topic at **http://www.usingenglish.com/handouts**.

- ProLiteracy's EdNet website may also have grammar material relevant to your lesson. The website is **http://www.proliteracyednet.org**.

Substitution Drills (high-beginning, intermediate)

PURPOSE

To provide practice using personal pronouns in prepositional phrases.

METHOD

You can use this substitution drill if you have already taught the object pronouns (e.g., *me, you, him, her, it*) and are now doing an activity that requires students to use them. If you find that they are having difficulty using the pronouns during the activity, stop and do the substitution drill. Then return to the activity, and give the students another opportunity to use the pronouns.

1. Say the following sentence, and ask the students to repeat it:
   "Throw the ball to me."

2. Say the pronoun and repeat the sentence:
   "*Me.* Throw the ball to me."

3. Ask the students to say the sentence again.

4. Say another pronoun and substitute it in the same sentence:
   "*Him.* Throw the ball to him."

5. Ask the students to repeat the new sentence.

6. Say another pronoun as a cue word: *"Her."*

7. Ask (or gesture for) a student to say the same sentence, substituting the new pronoun: "Throw the ball to her."

8. Do a random review with the other students. Say the cue word, and have a student say the sentence using that word.

SUGGESTION

- You can practice substitution drills with other slightly more challenging items. For example:

    (I/You/He/She/We/They) work/works downtown.

    (I/You/He/She/We/They) have/has a car.

    (I/You/He/She/We/They) don't/doesn't like snow.

    Put it/them on the table. (For this example, you can refer to objects such as the keys, the pen, the gloves, the book.)

If I Won the Lottery (intermediate, advanced)

PURPOSE

To review present *unreal* conditional sentences and to give students a break in the lesson as they imagine something they might like to do. (The present *unreal* conditional refers to a situation that is contrary to fact or not the case. The speaker is imagining what would happen if the situation were different from what actually is.)

METHOD

1. Tell the students that you want to talk about the state lottery. Bring in a lottery ad to aid the discussion. Show the ad and talk about what it says. Confirm that they understand what a lottery is.

2. Facilitate a discussion about the lottery—how often drawings occur and the amounts of money that can be won, if you know.

3. Read or tell a story about someone who actually won a lottery.

4. Tell the students that you want them to imagine that they have won the lottery: "Can you imagine winning the state lottery? What would you do if you won the lottery?"

5. Have them try to visualize for a minute what it would be like to win the lottery.

6. Share your own thoughts, using the conditional clause, "If I won the lottery, I would. . . ." This will help get the ball rolling as well as demonstrate the appropriate language. Remind them that they have recently learned the *If/I would* construction.

7. Invite a student to share his or her thoughts. Tell students to use the same conditional clause. Provide help if needed.

8. Provide students with other examples of the *If/would* expression:
   If Bill asked Helen to marry him, she would say yes.
   If my brother visited us at Christmas, I would be very happy.

SUGGESTIONS

- If you would prefer not to talk about the lottery with students, you can adapt this activity by simply asking them what they would do if they had a million dollars.

- You can use follow-up questions to extend both the discussion and the language practice.

   For example, a student might say,
      "If I won the lottery, I would travel around the world."

   You could then ask,
      "How long would your trip last?"
      "What kinds of transportation would you use?"
      "Would you take anyone else with you?"
      "What countries would you visit?"

   If you are working with a small group or class, you can involve other students, too, with questions such as these:
      "Who else would like to go on this trip?"
      "What countries would you visit, [Name]?"

- It may help to write down the students' responses and work together to revise the grammar as needed.

Conversation

ESL students need to have conversations with English speakers almost every day in a variety of community settings—settings such as the doctor's office, the supermarket, the post office, or their children's school. Tutors and teachers need to be aware of students' living, work, and family situations to identify the particular settings where they most need or want to use conversational English. Tutors and teachers also need to find out about the students' future work-related or educational goals to develop conversation activities that will help them in their daily lives.

The activities described in this section are specially designed to teach conversation. They all provide valuable practice and give students a chance to hear and feel how everyday language works. These can help give even very beginning students confidence that they will be able to participate in basic conversations.

Dialogues and role plays are two of the most useful activities for teaching conversation skills.

Dialogues (see Activity 12) are brief scripts related to everyday tasks such as asking for directions, asking what something costs, or sending a package at the post office. Dialogues are very good for general practice. They provide students with "stock phrases" to use in conversation. They also give valuable practice in initiating, steering, and concluding conversations. Being able to ask questions in conversation enables students to be proactive about getting their needs met. They no longer have to sit and wait for someone else to ask a question or start the conversation, as happens in many ESL classrooms.

Role plays (see Activity 13) can be natural extensions of dialogues. A role play allows students to go beyond a set script and begin using words and ideas more spontaneously. Role plays give students a nonthreatening way to practice real-life communication tasks such as speaking to a doctor, a child's teacher, a landlord, or a supervisor. You can also role-play telephone conversations. When students mention real-life conversational situations that are difficult for them, you can set up role plays and offer any relevant vocabulary and stock phrases that might be useful in that context.

Activity 12

Dialogues—Basic Steps
(high-beginning, intermediate, advanced)

PURPOSE

To give students initial practice using English in situations similar to those they will encounter in daily life.

METHOD

Prepare

1. Work with students to identify a setting or situation in which they need to be able to use English (e.g., a post office).

2. Identify one activity that commonly takes place in that setting (buying stamps). Do not try to focus on every possible interaction that could take place there.

3. Decide who the two people in the dialogue will be (postal clerk and customer).

4. Decide how long the dialogue will be. Three complete exchanges are about right for beginners. At this level, dialogues should be simple and brief.

5. Write the dialogue. Depending on the students' level, you can work with them to create a dialogue. To save time (or if you think they would not have the vocabulary to help create the dialogue), you can write it in advance.

   Here is an example of a post office dialogue:

Postal clerk:	Next!
Customer:	I'd like ten stamps, please.
Postal clerk:	What kind?
Customer:	Forever stamps.
Postal clerk:	That'll be [total cost].
Customer:	Thank you.

6. Decide what props or pictures you will need for teaching the dialogue (e.g., pictures of the inside and outside of a post office, forever stamps, several one-dollar bills, and the change you will need). Props and pictures are especially important to help beginning students envision the setting for the dialogue. With more advanced students, you can establish the setting verbally.

Pre-teach

7. Pre-teach any new vocabulary words the students will need to know (*next, stamps, forever*).

8. Pre-teach any new grammatical structures students will need to know (*I'd like . . .*).

Teach the dialogue to one student

9. Recite the whole dialogue (both parts) two to three times.

   As you say each part, move back and forth physically between the two imaginary positions of the speakers in the dialogue. This visual cue will help students differentiate between the two roles. Also use whatever props are necessary to indicate the nature of the conversation between the two speakers.

10. Take the first role; have the student take the second role.

11. Reverse roles with the student.

Involve other students

12. If you are in a small-group or classroom setting, call on another student to do the same dialogue with you. Repeat steps 1–3, using two students in the dialogue.

13. Call on two students to practice the dialogue with each other.

SUGGESTIONS

- Another example of a dialogue is a common greeting:

Person A: Hello. How are you?

Person B: Fine, thanks. How are you?

Person A: Fine, thanks.

- You can "recycle" dialogues you have already taught by rewriting them to add more detail. For example, in the case of the post office dialogue, the customer could buy international stamps in addition to the forever stamps or could mail a package.

- If you find dialogues in ESL texts that seem promising but are too long or complicated, you can rewrite them to make them simpler.

- If you know you'll be working on a dialogue in an upcoming class and the setting is a place you commonly visit (e.g., the post office, a restaurant, or a supermarket), you can listen for common phrases a student might hear in those settings. Try to incorporate those phrases into your dialogue.

- You can work with students to write dialogues on topics that you are studying. It's a great way to measure the language they already know and build on it.

- Telephone conversations are great practice for dialogues. You can practice how to handle wrong number calls, telemarketers, and more.

Activity 13

Role Plays
(high-beginning, intermediate, advanced)

PURPOSES

To give students an opportunity to use newly learned words and expressions in conversation in a nonthreatening environment.

To increase students' confidence in their ability to use English to meet their needs in the outside world.

METHOD

1. Teach a basic dialogue related to a specific situation (see Activity 12).

2. Explain that you'll practice the dialogue in a setting a little more like real life. Pass out any props needed for the role play. Stand up while you do the role play with a student.

3. Take the role of the first speaker. Say the same line you practiced in the dialogue. Then beckon the student to give the next line.

4. Modify your second line of the dialogue slightly to see how the student will respond. Example from the post office dialogue:

Postal clerk:	Next!
Customer:	I'd like ten stamps, please.
Postal clerk:	Forever stamps?
Customer:	Yes.
Postal clerk:	Did you say ten?
Customer:	Yes, please.
Postal clerk:	That's [total price].
Customer:	Thank you.

5. Practice again, modifying the dialogue even more. Example:

Postal clerk:	Next!
Customer:	I'd like ten stamps, please.
Postal clerk:	What kind of stamps? U.S. or international?
Customer:	U.S.
Postal clerk:	Ten forever stamps?
Customer:	Yes, please.
Postal clerk:	That'll be [total price].
Customer:	Thank you.

6. If the students seem comfortable with role plays, practice again, but have them modify what they say. Encourage them to be creative.

SUGGESTIONS

- In small-group situations, you can introduce a new character (yourself or another student) into the role play to challenge the other students to use their conversation skills to meet a changing situation. For example, the customer's neighbor enters the post office. The neighbor greets the customer and asks her where she's going after she leaves the post office.

- More advanced students can do role plays without the preliminary dialogue. You can simply pre-teach any vocabulary words you think are necessary and ask them to incorporate those words into the role play.

Activity 14

Using Picture Stories for Health Literacy (all)

PURPOSE

To encourage students to practice health vocabulary and discuss topics related to health and well-being.

METHOD

1. Have ready a copy of the picture on page 65, called "Stressed Out!!!"

2. Ask a student what is happening in the picture. Point to each frame to discuss it.

Ask level-appropriate questions to elicit specific details or observations. Here are some possible questions you might ask:

First frame: What time is it? Who is in the picture? What is her name? (You and the student can make up a name.) What is the mother doing? What is the baby doing? How does the mother feel?

Second frame: What time is it now? Who are the people in the picture? What do you think they want? Who makes breakfast for them? Where is the mother now?

Third frame: What time is it now? Where is [name]? What is the problem? Who is the man? What is he saying? Is he happy? Why or why not? How does [name] feel?

Fourth frame: What time is it now? Where do you think [name] is? What happened? How does she feel?

Fifth frame: What time is it now? Where do you think [name] is? What is she holding in her hand? What is she thinking? Is she happy?

Sixth frame: What time is it now? What is [name] doing? Why? What are the woman's problems in this story?

3. Ask students to suggest what the woman might do to lower the level of stress in her life. Ask them how or when they feel stress. You can discuss situations that are stressful for you and what you do to manage stress. Then ask the students what things are stressful for them and how they manage that stress.

SUGGESTION

- The story on page 65 comes from a series of health stories on topics such as nutrition, depression, emergencies, and domestic violence. For more picture stories, go to **http://www.cal.org/caela/esl_resources/Health/ healthindex.html**.

(Adapted from "Using Picture Stories for Health Literacy," *Notebook*, Spring 2008, pp. 3–5, ProLiteracy.)

STRESSED OUT!!!

(From Singleton, K. (2001). *Picture Stories for Adult ESL Health Literacy*. Available at Center for Applied Linguistics website. URL: **http://www.cal.org/caela/esl_resources/Health/healthindex.html**. Used with permission.)

Conversation Prompts (all)

PURPOSE

To engage in conversation on specific topics.

METHOD

There may be times in tutoring sessions when it will be appropriate to engage in casual conversation with a student. This might be a regular activity to build the student's fluency. It could be an appropriate approach with a student who needs extra work on speaking skills. You might also want to use casual conversation to extend practice on a subject you are studying. For example, if you are studying jobs, you might want to plan a structured conversation about a student's work goals.

1. Decide in advance what you will discuss. See page 67 for conversation prompts related to English learning, culture, music, and more. Focus on one topic at a time.

2. If students are at a lower proficiency level, supply them with copies of some leading questions. Although this makes the practice less authentic, it helps to pre-teach words they may not know. It also gives them time to think about the questions.

3. Use the leading questions to generate a conversation. Ask follow-up questions, and encourage the student to ask you follow-up questions. Five minutes or so of conversation might be enough for a beginning student. With an advanced student, the conversation may last for 10 or 15 minutes. Do not aim to correct speaking errors on the spot; instead, take note of errors you'd like to discuss after the activity.

4. Take some time after the conversation to go over new vocabulary words that came up or to identify patterns of errors you noticed (in pronunciation, word choice, or grammatical structures). Point out that asking follow-up questions is a great way to keep a conversation going, a valuable skill in many different social situations.

SUGGESTIONS

- These questions work with small groups or classes as well as with individual students.

- The questions also serve as great writing prompts.

SUGGESTED CONVERSATION TOPICS

General

What would you expect/like to be doing one year from now? Five years from now?

What were you doing one year ago? Five years ago? (These are good for practicing past and future tenses.)

Bring in an advice column. Read the problem. Ask participants what they think the writer should do. Then hand out the advice columnist's answer. Ask the students what they think of that advice.

What makes you happy/unhappy? (Discuss vocabulary for emotions: What makes you jealous, excited, discouraged, amused, relieved, disappointed, etc.?)

What person do you admire most? Why?

Tell the group about something that made a really big difference in your life.

U.S. Culture

Talk about U.S./American customs and usages.

Discuss accepted forms of introduction and address (formal and informal).

Preceding a federal/national holiday, a brief discussion of the significance of the date is often useful. This may include a short American history lesson and a discussion of customs.

Compare and contrast the United States/America with the home country.

Talk about housing, food, schools, government, etc.

Discuss how (or if) the United States/America is different from what may have been expected.

Vocabulary

When do you speak English? At home? During school? While shopping?

Do you keep a notebook to write down new words or ideas you have learned?

For vocabulary growth and enrichment, provide a list of ten new words for memorization and use, including proper pronunciation.

Discuss idioms and their meanings.

Use tongue twisters to practice pronunciation.

Practice numbers (e.g., 16 vs. 60, numbers in the thousands and millions).

Entertainment

Discuss current events, TV shows, movies, etc.

What do you like to do in your free time? Do you have a hobby?

What are you reading now? In what language?

What movies do you like? In what language?

What kind of music do you like? Why? Bring a CD to share with the group.

Tell something about the music you have brought.

Jobs and Job Hunting

Do you have special skills or training? What things do you think you can do better than most other people? Would you like to teach about these things?

Are you working or looking for work? Do you have a résumé?

Did you work in your home country? What did you do?

What questions will you be asked in an interview?

What is your dream job?

Analyze job ads.

Health

Talk about how to maintain good health. What is your "health literacy" in English?

Pretend to call 911 to respond to emergencies. Note: Local fire stations can send a trained EMS professional to talk to your class about emergencies.

How can you stay healthy? (Discuss healthy diet, exercise, stress reduction, etc.)

When should you go to the doctor (cold vs. flu, medical conditions, injuries, annual exams, etc.)?

Travel

What places would you like to visit in the United States? In the world? Why?

Discuss giving directions. Analyze a map.

Talk about transportation. How did you get to the United States (car, bus, plane, train, etc.)?

Do you prefer to fly or to drive? Why?

Are you planning a vacation? Where are you going?

Money

Do you have a bank account? Do you prefer to use cash, credit card, debit card, or checks? Why?

What would you do if you won the lottery? Is it better to save the money or spend the money? (This is a good way to practice or introduce the conditional tense.)

Discuss money and how much different things cost. Practice giving a price and making change.

Do you like to go shopping? Why? Where? Is shopping different in your home country?

Family

Tell the group about your family. Are you married? Do you have children?

Do you have pets? Did you have a pet in your home country?

Do you have a big family or a small family?

Are you the oldest, middle, youngest, or only child?

What family members are in the United States/your home country?

Housing

Do you live in a house or an apartment?

Discuss rooms in the house and furniture vocabulary.

Draw a floor plan, and give a tour of your house.

Where would you like to live?

Analyze housing ads.

Food

What is your favorite food?

What food do you see here that you never saw in your country?

What food do you eat in your country that you can't find here?

What food do you make for special occasions in your country?

What food do you like to cook?

Do you cook often? What will you eat tonight?

Do you think food in the United States is better or worse than food in your country? (Often, students answer that food is faster to make but less healthy and tasty.)

Adapted from the *Literacy Council of Northern Virginia's Conversation Class Handbook.* Published by the Literacy Council of Northern Virginia. Revised August 2007. Used with permission. For a copy of the handbook, email Erin Finn at EFinn@LCNV.org.

Native Country

What is one of the best things about your native country?

What is a problem in your country?

Who is a famous person in your country? Why is he or she famous?

What is a national holiday in your country?

What is the weather like in your country?

What interesting places do tourists visit in your country?

Music

What kind of music do you like?

What are your favorite music groups or performers? Why do you like them?

When do you like to listen to music?

When do you listen to traditional songs from your country?

Can you play any musical instruments? When and how did you learn?

Have You Ever...? Explain.

Have you ever been in the newspaper?

Have you ever done something dangerous?

Have you ever helped a stranger?

Have you ever been on TV?

Have you ever quit a bad habit?

Suggested by Christine Polk.

Newspapers as a Cultural Key
(intermediate, advanced)

PURPOSE

To use newspaper classified ads as a way to stimulate discussions about cross-cultural behaviors. (This activity works best in a small-group or classroom setting.)

METHOD

1. In advance, save copies of classified ads in your local paper, or find and print relevant ads online. You will need one set of ads for each person, but they do not have to be from the same day's paper.

2. Highlight the section headings on each student's copy.

3. Divide the students into groups of three. For each group, prepare a different card related to one of the section headings. Put the section heading on the front of the card. On the back, write questions designed to stimulate discussion about cultural issues related to that section. Examples:

Merchandise

In your country:

- Do people advertise things for sale in the newspaper?
- If so, is there a fixed price, or do people bargain?

Do Americans bargain?

Roommates

In your country:

- Do strangers share apartments?
- Do young men and women live on their own before they get married?

What do you think about some Americans who live away from their families before they are married?

Employment

In your country:

- Do employers advertise their jobs in the paper?
- Do people usually get jobs by knowing someone important?

How do you think Americans find jobs?

Pets

In your country:

- Do people buy and sell pets?
- What are some common pets in your country?

What do you think about Americans and their pets?

4. Give each group one of the cards and three copies of the classified ads.

5. Ask each group to do the following:

   a. Look for the section of the classified ads that matches the name on the front of the card.

   b. Read some of the ads under that heading to each other.

   c. Discuss the questions on the back of the card.

6. After the groups have had a chance to complete their discussions, call on each group to report what they discussed. Open the discussion to the rest of the class. After a minute or two of follow-up discussion, clarify for everyone the way Americans might handle any of the issues that have come up.

SUGGESTIONS

- You can mix students from different countries in each of the small groups. This will make for more interesting discussion.

- You can also do this activity with the whole group rather than with small groups. Read the card to the group, and then let them discuss the questions. You can then report on the activity in different lessons, using one card each time.

- Other sections of the newspaper can also be used to point out and discuss American cultural behavior (e.g., personal advice columns, store advertisements, or the comics).

Activity 17

Role Play—Finding an Apartment
(high-beginning, intermediate, advanced)

PURPOSE

To give students speaking practice in the context of looking for an apartment.

METHOD

1. Have students look at the classified ads shown on page 72. (Have copies of this page ready in advance.) As an alternative, you can find apartment rental ads from your newspaper in advance and show those instead.

2. Tell students to imagine that a friend from their country has just arrived in the United States and that they need to help the friend find a place to live. The apartment must be near a bus route and have laundry facilities. Brainstorm

with students a list of things the friend might want to know about the apartment before he or she would sign a lease.

3. Have students use the list of suggested questions below to practice making "phone calls" to ask for details about each apartment listing. For additional practice, students can practice arranging a time to see the apartment. Play the role of rental agent, and answer questions about the apartment.

> Location?
> Near bus?
> Heat/hot water included?
>
> Available now?
> Laundry?
> Appointment?

4. As you perform role plays, note ways that the participating student might improve pronunciation, sentence structure, and word choices to be understood better. Also think about social/conversational conventions that might make the interaction go more smoothly.

5. Encourage students to incorporate these suggestions as you role-play calls about the other two ads.

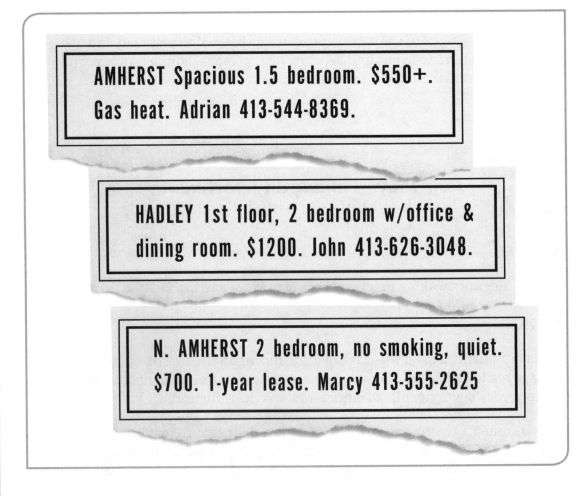

AMHERST Spacious 1.5 bedroom. $550+.
Gas heat. Adrian 413-544-8369.

HADLEY 1st floor, 2 bedroom w/office &
dining room. $1200. John 413-626-3048.

N. AMHERST 2 bedroom, no smoking, quiet.
$700. 1-year lease. Marcy 413-555-2625

Conversation Activities for Small Groups and Classes

The following activities are helpful to use in small groups and classes. They allow students to boost their confidence in less structured, spontaneous conversation.

Activity 18 — *Question Strips* (all)

PURPOSE

To enable students to initiate conversation on a variety of topics. (This activity is especially useful if the students in your group are at different language skill levels.)

METHOD

1. Make a list of several questions, and put them on strips of paper. Write one question per strip. Examples:

    a. When was the last time you went to a movie?

    b. Have you ever met a famous person? Who?

    c. What is your favorite food? Why?

2. Distribute one question strip to each student.

3. Tell students to walk around and find partners. Have the partners ask each other the questions they have on their strips. Students should not show their written questions to their partners. That would defeat the purpose of the activity.

4. After they have answered each other's questions, tell them to trade questions, find new partners, and repeat the process.

5. Continue the activity until students have partnered with each person in the group or until interest starts to diminish.

SUGGESTIONS

*   Select topics that interest the students. This encourages them to respond more fully.

*   Avoid questions on topics that students might consider private or inappropriate for discussion because of their cultural backgrounds. Similarly, avoid questions that are viewed by Americans as private or inappropriate for public discussion.

- Try to phrase the questions using grammatical structures and vocabulary that are familiar to most of the students.

- Use questions that are likely to give the questioner *new information.* In natural conversation, people don't ask questions if they already know the answers. For example, questions such as "Where do you live?" or "Do you have any brothers or sisters?" create real communication only if the questioner does *not* already have that information.

- Remember that the way you phrase a question can either encourage or limit discussion. With a low-level group, questions that call for one-word or very short answers might be enough. Example: "Do you like ice cream?"

- If you have a multilevel class, encourage the more proficient students to help the lower-level ESL students by reading their questions for them.

- To simulate a real-life interaction, encourage students to follow up on answers by adding their own comments ("Oh, really? That's my favorite food, too.") or by asking questions to get additional information ("What was the name of the movie? How did you like it?"). Such discussion helps students focus on what's being discussed rather than on how it is being said.

- With a more advanced group, encourage discussion or extended answers by including one or more follow-up questions on the strip. Example: "What was [famous person] like?"

- Use question strips to help people learn some of the English conversational conventions that go along with question-and-answer exchanges. Examples:

How to approach a stranger and initiate conversation:

"Excuse me, may I ask you something?"

How to lead up to a question that is culturally acceptable but might seem personal or a bit awkward:

"I hope you don't mind my asking, but . . ."

How to avoid answering a question if the person being asked feels that it's too personal:

"I'm sorry, but I'd rather not discuss that."

How to ask for clarification:

"Could you explain that?"

"I'm not exactly sure what you mean."

How to acknowledge what somebody says:

"Really?"

"I see."

"Tell me more about that."

Find Someone Who...
(high-beginning, intermediate, advanced)

PURPOSE

To give students practice asking questions in an informal conversational setting.

METHOD

1. Give students a copy of the handout on the following page.

2. Ask students to walk around and find at least one person who fits into each category. Have them write down the name of that person.

3. Debrief as a group. Ask questions (or have students ask questions) to find out more information. Example: "Juan says he is a morning person. Juan, what time do you wake up?"

(Activity courtesy of the Jones Library, Amherst, Massachusetts.)

Find Someone Who ...

1. Has kept a garden   1. _____

2. Has met a celebrity from his or her native   2. _____
   country. Who was it?

3. Knows an identical twin   3. _____

4. Is a morning person   4. _____

5. Is a pessimist   5. _____

6. Does not know how to swim   6. _____

7. Has met his or her great-great-   7. _____
   grandmother

8. Is a vegetarian   8. _____

9. Has more than five siblings   9. _____

10. Heard about this class through a friend   10. _____

Find Someone Who ...

1. Has kept a garden   1. _____

2. Has met a celebrity from his or her native   2. _____
   country. Who was it?

3. Knows an identical twin   3. _____

4. Is a morning person   4. _____

5. Is a pessimist   5. _____

6. Does not know how to swim   6. _____

7. Has met his or her great-great-   7. _____
   grandmother

8. Is a vegetarian   8. _____

9. Has more than five siblings   9. _____

10. Heard about this class through a friend   10. _____

(Activity courtesy of the Jones Library, Amherst, Massachusetts.)

Activity 20

Who Am I? (intermediate, advanced)

PURPOSE

To give students an opportunity to practice questions and answers.

METHOD

1. Write the names of famous people on 3" × 5" cards, one name per card. Prepare one card per student. Consider that students may not be aware of people who are famous only in the United States. Choose people who are recognized internationally, such as Michael Jackson, Arnold Schwarznegger, and the current U.S. president. Include a picture of the person with each card, if possible.

2. Stick one card on each student's back with adhesive tape.

3. Have students stand up and form pairs. In each pair, the first student reads (silently) the name on the second student's back. The second student's task is to find out his or her own "identity" by asking the first student yes-or-no questions. When the second student guesses the right answer, they switch roles.

4. Then have students form different pairs and repeat the activity.

SUGGESTIONS

*   Be sure to select names of people the students will be likely to know.

*   For beginning students, you can use pictures of famous people instead of writing their names.

*   The first time you try this activity, students may be somewhat shy or reluctant. Circulate around the room to help and encourage them.

*   Use your own judgment about how long to let the activity continue. If the students seem to be enjoying themselves and are actively involved in discussion, keep things going.

Activity 21

"Liars" (intermediate, advanced)

PURPOSES

To give students practice with questions and answers.

To prompt students to engage in somewhat fast conversations in English.

METHOD

1. Tell students that they will be playing a game called "Liars."

2. Ask them if they know what the word *liars* means. Explain if necessary.

3. Before beginning the activity, model it for the students. Tell them three things about yourself. Explain that one of the three things is a lie. Tell students to ask you questions to help them identify the lie. Give them a few minutes to ask their questions. Then ask them to guess which statement is a lie. If they don't guess correctly, tell them the answer.

4. Tell the students that each of them will have a chance to be a liar. Give them a few minutes to sit quietly and think of three statements. One must be a lie. Have them write the statements in preparation for the activity.

5. Form groups of three students each. Ask each group to pick the first speaker.

6. Give each group three minutes to listen to the speaker's statements and ask questions.

7. Signal them when three minutes are up. Ask each group to guess which statement is the lie.

8. Repeat steps 6–7 for each member of the group.

9. At the end of this part of the activity, ask each group to choose the person that they think did the best job of fooling the other members of the group. Then have these people try to fool the rest of the class. Once again, invite the other students to ask questions of the liar. (The members of the person's original group should not participate.)

SUGGESTIONS

- When preparing to model your own statements, choose true statements that might seem hard for the students to believe and a lie that seems plausible—making your lie more difficult to guess. This will show students the approach they should take.

- It is best to do this activity after students have gotten to know each other, rather than during the first few ESL sessions. The fun is in trying to determine the truth based on what students already think they know about each other.

- You may choose to vary the time allotted for the activity, but you should give a time limit of some sort so that students will work quickly.

What's Missing? (beginning)

PURPOSE

To have students practice using questions and answers and asking for clarification.

METHOD

1. Put students in groups of three.

2. Give each group member a picture. The basic pictures are the same, but for each student, a couple of items (different for each one) will be missing. You can use the pictures on the next page or create your own sets of pictures.

3. Put the pictures in file folders so group members can see only their own versions.

4. Tell students that their task is to talk among themselves to determine what is missing from their own pictures and then to draw in the missing items. The goal is for all the students to end up with the same complete picture. An example dialogue might go something like this:

Student A:	Is there a dog?
Student B:	Yes. There is a dog beside the bus stop.
Student A:	My picture does not have a dog. There is a man with a bag and a woman with a child.
Student C:	My picture has a man and a bag and a woman but no child.

TEACHING ADULTS: AN ESL RESOURCE BOOK

5. When the students have completed their task, go over the results with them: "What differences did you find?"

SUGGESTIONS

- Create your own sets of images. Use simple line drawings. Children's coloring books are excellent for this. Determine which items can be eliminated in each version. Use correction fluid to blank out those items before photocopying each of the versions.

- For a follow-up activity, have students write down all the items that they can find in their pictures. Or have them write descriptive paragraphs about their pictures.

- For low-beginning students, simplify the task. Work with a category of items—for example, fruits. Give each student the same drawing of several fruits, but remove a different fruit from each drawing. The task for each student is to find out through discussion which fruit is missing (without looking at other pictures). The last step is to draw the missing fruit in its correct place.

- Check out similar activities that are available online. Search for "find the difference," "spot the difference," or "what's wrong with the picture."

(Adapted from a presentation given by Sue Goldstein.)

Activity 23 *Meeting and Greeting—Conversation Practice* (all)

PURPOSE

To give students practice introducing themselves and engaging in conversation with new acquaintances.

METHOD

1. Review with students some expressions or phrases used when meeting someone for the first time. Examples:

> "Hello, my name is _____."
> (A handshake is appropriate for this and either of the following.)
> "Hello, nice to meet you. My name is _____."
> "Hello, how are you? My name is _____."

2. Review some of the expressions or phrases used to close a conversation. Examples:

> "It was nice meeting you."
> (A handshake is appropriate for this and any of the following.)
> "It was nice to meet you. I hope we'll meet again."
> "Oh, look at the time. I have to go. It was nice to meet you."
> "Would you excuse me, please? I enjoyed talking with you about _____."

3. Describe a scenario in which they might have to introduce themselves in a social setting. For example, they are all at a party being sponsored by the ESL program. The party is an opportunity to meet ESL students and teachers from other classes.

4. Write the following words where the students can see them:

> Where from?   Your job?
> How long in United States?   Anything else?

Using simple phrases as stimuli instead of complete questions prevents students from memorizing the exact wording of the questions to be asked.

5. Ask students to stand up and walk around as though they were at a party. They should imagine that they do not know anyone else at the party. They are to approach each other and introduce themselves. They should ask questions based on the words on the chalkboard. They can also talk about other things if they choose to do so. Finally, they should end the conversation and move away to find someone else to meet and talk with.

SUGGESTIONS

- Decide how much pre-teaching or practicing of the opening and closing expressions is needed. Give beginning students the opportunity to practice the expressions in role plays before they do this activity.

- Once the activity starts, let students engage freely in conversation. Tell them not to worry about how correct they are in their use of these expressions. The same pertains to the questions they ask each other.

The Sounds of English

Students who have an extensive English vocabulary and a good grasp of English grammar might still be unable to speak the language so that others can understand them. To be understood, a speaker needs to pronounce individual English sounds (phonemes) correctly. The speaker also needs to use appropriate English patterns of stress, rhythm, and intonation.

Here are some helpful guidelines for teaching both sounds and patterns:

- Keep sessions short. This type of practice can become tedious.

- Use lots of repetition. Recycle sounds and patterns from one session to the next.

- Use familiar vocabulary. Don't introduce new English vocabulary or structures during this part of the lesson.

- Help students recognize everyday pronunciation and patterns as well as "textbook pronunciation" and patterns. This helps students become familiar with the English they will actually hear in the outside world. Examples: "I gotta go now." "Hower you today?"

- Encourage students to use digital recorders during pronunciation lessons to remember difficult sounds.

- In addition to pronunciation-focused textbooks, check out some good websites that offer pronunciation practice. One such site is The Sounds of American English (**http://www.uiowa.edu/~acadtech/phonetics/english/frameset.html**).

- Teach pronunciation and patterns in meaningful contexts rather than in isolation. For example, if a Spanish speaker is having difficulty making the /i/ sound, as in *bit*, practice a sentence or dialogue that includes words with this sound.

> "Excuse me. Which aisle are the potato chips in?"
> "Potato chips are in aisle six."

When doing activities focused on meaning or communication, do not stop to make a correction unless you cannot understand what a student is saying—students are generally trying hard to focus on meaning during an ESL lesson. Instead, make notes about a student's difficulties with individual sounds or with patterns. Pay special attention to problems with patterns. Then set aside a separate time to work on these items.

Teaching Individual Sounds

Sounds are not the same as letters. Some letters have more than one sound: for example, *c*, as in *city* and *cup*. Some sounds can be represented in English by different letters or letter combinations: for example, *fix, phone, cough*. The section that follows focuses on the *sounds* of the language, not the letters used to represent those sounds.

This book uses italics to indicate the name of a letter: *b*. It uses slashes to indicate the sound of a letter: /b/. A macron over a letter indicates a long vowel sound: /ā/. A single vowel has a short sound if there is no macron: /a/. Capital letters show a word or part of a word that is stressed: WORKshop.

There are three major reasons why students have problems with individual sounds:

1. The sound is new to the student.

   For example, a French speaker learning English is apt to have difficulty with a word like *thank* because French has no /th/ sound. A French speaker tends to say *sank* or *tank* instead.

2. The sound exists in the student's native language but comes in a place that is new to him or her.

   For example, an English speaker learning Vietnamese is apt to have difficulty with words like *Nganh* and *Nguyen*. Although English has the /ng/ sound, it does not have that sound at the beginning of words. A Cambodian learning English will tend to drop final /s/ sounds because the Khmer language does not have an /s/ sound at the end of words. The English words *bus* and *peace* might become *buh* and *pea*.

3. The sound doesn't exist in the student's native language but is similar to one that does.

   For example, a Spanish speaker learning English is apt to have difficulty distinguishing between the vowel sounds in the words *bit* and *beet*. The Spanish sound system has the /ē/ sound but not the /i/ sound, so Spanish speakers tend to say both these words with the /ē/ sound.

You can teach sounds in three ways. You can ask students to listen while you model the sound yourself, you can have them watch your mouth as you make the sound, or you can describe how you are using your tongue, lips, throat, and the flow of air to make the sound. Students can look at their mouths in a mirror or touch their mouths as they practice different sounds.

Listed on the next page are some examples of terms for describing both what is happening in the mouth and what the key features of individual sounds are. Appendix A (page 172) contains a list of English speech sounds and their descriptions.

Continuant/Stop

If you can continue the sound as long as you want, it's a continuant. If the sound just stops, it's a stop. Some of the consonant sounds, such as /s/, /m/, and /l/, are continuants, as are all the vowel sounds. The consonant sounds /b/, /p/, and /t/ are examples of stops.

Voiced/Unvoiced

If you use your vocal cords when you make the sound, it's voiced. All the vowel sounds are voiced. If you don't use your vocal cords, the sound is unvoiced. Some consonant sounds, such as /z/, are voiced. Others, such as /s/, are unvoiced.

Nasal

If the sound comes from your nose, it's a nasal sound. The sounds /m/, /n/, and /ng/ are nasal sounds.

Front/Back

Vowels can be described by the place in the mouth where the tongue "humps" up. An example of a "front vowel" sound is /ē/, as in *feel*. For this sound, the hump is at the front of the mouth. An example of a "back vowel" sound is /oo/ as in *tool*. For this sound, the hump is at the back of the mouth.

Tense/Lax

Vowels can be described by the degree of tenseness or laxness of the muscles of the mouth. For example, the /ē/ sound in the word *cheap* makes the mouth feel more tense than the /i/ sound in the word *chip*, although the position of the mouth is almost the same for each of these sounds. Thus, the sound /ē/ (tense) and /i/ (lax) form a tense/lax pair.

Rounded/Unrounded

Vowels can also be described by the degree of rounding of the lips during production of the sound. All front vowels are made with lips unrounded (e.g., /ē/, /i/, /a/). All back vowels are made with rounded lips (e.g., /oo/, /ō/).

Vowel Length

Vowel sounds have different lengths, or durations, depending on whether a voiced or an unvoiced consonant follows the vowel or whether the vowel falls at the end of the word. The vowel sound is shortest when an unvoiced consonant follows the vowel (*seat*). It is longer when a voiced consonant follows the vowel (*seed*). It is longer when the vowel sound is at the end of the word (*see*).

Activity 24

Minimal Pairs (beginning)

PURPOSE

To help students hear the difference between two sounds (listening) and then correctly produce each of the sounds (speaking). (A minimal pair consists of two words that differ only in one sound, e.g., *hat/bat, rake/rate, hit/heat.*)

METHOD

1. Identify the two sounds you want to work on, for example, /l/ and /r/.

2. Create a list of words that contrast these two sounds. Make sure that the two sounds you are focusing on are the only differences between the two words. For example, *lip* and *hip* would be a minimal pair. You can search online for minimal pair lists ideal for ESL teaching.

    Here is an example of a minimal pair list for /l/ and /r/.

/l/	/r/
lip	rip
lock	rock
lap	rap
late	rate

3. Create flashcards for the two sounds you have chosen, as shown on the next page.

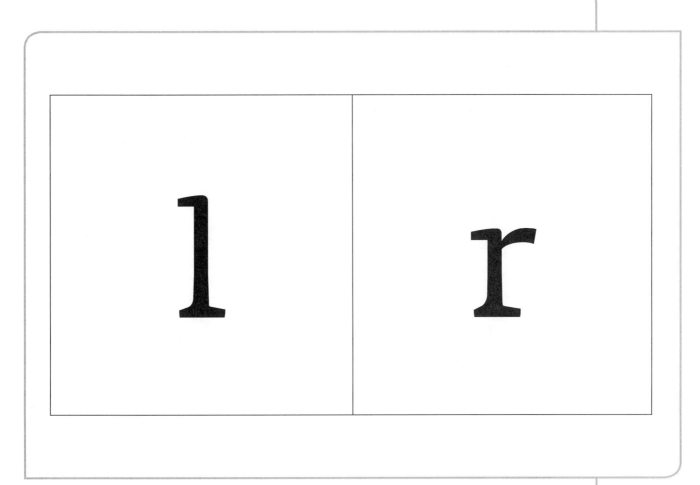

4. Ask the student to listen to the difference between the two sounds as you say first one and then the other (first the /l/ sound and then the /r/ sound).

5. Ask the student to listen to the difference again. This time, as you pronounce the /l/ sound, raise the *l* flashcard. As you pronounce the /r/ sound, raise the *r* flashcard.

6. Read the first pair of words on the list (*lip/rip*). After you read each word, ask the student to point to one of the flashcards to indicate which sound the word begins with. If a student has difficulty, demonstrate by saying each word again and raising the appropriate flashcard.

7. Repeat the process with the first few pairs on the list.

8. When a student understands what to do, begin alternating between reading the /l/ word first or the /r/ word first.

9. Go back through the list, and have the student repeat the words in pairs after you.

10. Finally, put the words into a meaningful context so the student has an opportunity to practice saying the two sounds in sentences.

SUGGESTIONS

- Instead of flashcards, raise one finger for the first sound and two fingers for the second sound. Have the student raise one or two fingers depending on the number that corresponds to the sound.

- If possible, use pictures for the final step when introducing the sentences.

Reading and Writing

Students naturally will need to read and sometimes write a variety of items in their everyday lives. This can include job applications, doctor or hospital forms, memos, emails, text messages, reports, and notes to a child's school office.

By one definition, *reading* is *a process for deriving meaning from text.* To be successful in this process, a reader must

- use effective eye movement.

- have a large enough listening and speaking vocabulary to be able to match the printed word to the spoken word.

- understand the basic structure (grammar) of the language.

- have some prior experience or knowledge about the topic.

- have strategies for interacting with the text, such as predicting/confirming and identifying cause and effect.

- know the "code": the sounds of English letters and letter combinations.

By one definition, *writing* is *the ability to make the written symbols that form the alphabet.* But writing is also *a process for communicating meaning through print.*

Literacy Skills—Where Do Your Students Fit?

Some students will not be able to read or write in their native languages. This makes learning reading and writing in English much harder. Other students are fully literate in their native languages and may even have advanced degrees. The following chart, published in 2003 by the Center for Adult English Language Acquisition, presents categories of students who may be in ESL classes. It may help you to know where your students fit so you can adjust your teaching accordingly. You can find a longer version of the chart and more information on working with literacy-level students at **http://www.cal.org/caela/esl_resources/digests/litQA.html**.

Preliterate: The native language does not yet have a writing system.

Nonliterate: The native language has a written form, but the student has no literacy.

Semiliterate: The student has minimal literacy in his or her native language.

Nonalphabet literate: The student is literate in a language that is not alphabetic (e.g., Chinese).

Non-Roman alphabet literate: The student is literate in an alphabetic language that does not use the Roman alphabet (e.g., Arabic, Russian).

Roman-alphabet literate: The student is literate in a language that is written in the Roman alphabet (e.g., Spanish, German).

Principles of Teaching Reading and Writing

Here are some general principles to keep in mind when teaching reading and writing to ESL students.

Consider what adults bring to the learning setting.

Adult ESL students may not be able to speak English very well, and some may be unable to read in any language. But remember that they bring with them a lifetime of other knowledge and experience acquired from their families, friends, communities, jobs, religious institutions, schooling, travels, and more. As an ESL tutor or teacher, you might find yourself working with a farmer who has years of experience growing rice, a seamstress who supports a family of five with her sewing skills, a fisherman who has extensive knowledge of marine life, or a midwife who was the sole health care provider in a small rural village.

You can build on students' rich backgrounds by respecting their experiences and encouraging them to share these experiences in class. Always be on the lookout for teaching materials that relate to a student's life skills and interests. In this way, you will be validating and affirming him or her as a fellow adult.

Teach new words orally first . . .

People should learn the meanings of words by hearing and speaking them before trying to read them. This is especially important with beginning-level students. Decoding new words in print can be difficult unless a student is already familiar with the meaning orally.

. . . but introduce reading and writing as soon as possible.

Educators don't necessarily agree on when to introduce reading and writing. Those who favor exposing nonliterate adults to print from the beginning give the following reasons:

- Most students equate education with reading and writing. Reading and writing activities can be highly motivating for them.

- To function effectively in their everyday lives, students need to be able to recognize important print words such as *in, out, push, pull, men,* and *women.* They also need to be able to write their names and addresses.

- Reading and writing are very useful for reinforcing the language skills that students are acquiring through listening and speaking.

- People's learning styles are different. Some people learn better or retain information better by seeing and doing (reading and writing) than by listening and speaking alone.

- Reading and writing are effective tools that students can use to acquire the information they need.

Establish a context for reading.

ESL students will encounter many words in print that are unfamiliar to them. Being able to sound out or decode a word will not help if a student does not know what the word means. Often he or she will be able to read enough words to figure out the general meaning of the passage. But sometimes, not knowing a word will make it almost impossible to get meaning from that particular text.

It is much more likely that students will be able to figure out the meaning of a word if they understand the context of the passage. They will also be better prepared to understand the author's message and relate it to their own ideas and experiences. There are several things that you can do to help create context for students:

- Use pictures to help bridge the gap between the information in the text and the students' own knowledge and experiences. For example, some students might not recognize the word *spider.* Such students would be thoroughly confused if they tried to read an article about spiders. An accompanying picture of spiders can provide the needed context, enable students to access their store of background knowledge about spiders, and help them narrow down the possibilities when they come to unfamiliar words.

- Use pre-reading activities (described later in this chapter) to help provide context and allow students to share what they already know about the topic.

- Use the Language Experience Approach (LEA) described in this chapter. In LEA, a student talks about an experience or an idea, and you write down the words. What you have written becomes the reading text. In this case, you don't have to worry about creating context for the student. The context is already there!

- Keep reading and writing practical. Supplement stories that you read in class with forms and instructions you commonly find at the library, in doctor's offices, at the bank, at the Department of Motor Vehicles, and in employment offices. Encourage your students to bring in paperwork that they receive as well. Then you can review it with them. This might include bills, memos from work, and notices from a child's school.

Start with printing.

You may find yourself working with students who cannot read or write in their own language or whose native language uses a writing system different from that of English (e.g., Chinese, Thai, Arabic, or Hindi). Such students will first need to learn to write the letters of the English alphabet. In most cases, the best place to start is with printing (manuscript writing) rather than with cursive writing. Here are some reasons for this:

- It is more similar to the print that students will see in books, magazines, and newspapers.

- Most forms that students will need to fill out in daily life require the use of printing.

Use writing to reinforce reading.

As students learn to read new words, idioms, everyday expressions, and stock phrases, give them an opportunity to write the words as well. Writing reinforces the meanings of new words and expressions.

Focus on content, not correctness.

People learn to speak by speaking, to read by reading, and to write by writing. Mistakes will be a natural part of that learning process. When people are learning to write, help them focus on the *message they are trying to communicate* rather than on perfectly formed letters, correct spelling, and perfect grammar. This is especially important with beginning students.

One way to help students who may be nervous about their writing ability is to encourage them to write the way they speak. This advice is equally useful for beginning-level ESL students who can already read and write in their native languages and for those who have never written in any language. As students become more comfortable with both English and writing, you can focus more attention on correctness.

Encourage students to keep personal dictionaries.

A personal dictionary will help reinforce new vocabulary. Your students can create special notebooks where they write new words and add short definitions. You'll probably find that beginning students want to include translations of the words as well. In addition to the words they work on with you, encourage students to add words that they learn outside of class to their dictionaries. You can take time during class/tutoring sessions to review previous vocabulary and answer any questions they may have.

Language Experience Approach

The Language Experience Approach (LEA) is a simple but powerful technique for teaching reading to beginning and intermediate students. It can be used with classes, with small groups, or in one-to-one tutoring. In an LEA activity, a student or group tells a story, and you write down the words as spoken. The story provides content for the reading lesson.

LEA builds on students' life experiences and treats them as adults with ideas, feelings, and stories that are worth communicating. The technique is especially effective because it encourages students to use all four basic language skills: listening, speaking, reading, and writing.

LEA gives students an opportunity to share what they know and to read something that they themselves have created. Other advantages of using LEA include the following:

- Students are more interested in learning to read if they can read their own words on topics of their own choosing.

- Students feel empowered because you show respect both for them and for their stories by writing the stories down.

- Students see the powerful connection between the spoken and written word. Although many people take this connection for granted, beginning readers may be discovering for the first time that printed words are really representations of spoken words.

Creating a Language Experience Story
(beginning, intermediate)

PURPOSE

To use materials created from a student's own words and life experiences as the basis for reading instruction.

METHOD

These instructions are written for a one-to-one tutoring situation, but the process can easily be adapted for use with a small group or a class.

1. Ask the student to tell you a brief story or to share an experience with you. Alternately, you can ask him or her to talk about a specific topic related to something you are teaching. See the box on page 95 for LEA story topic ideas.

2. Listen. Stop to ask for clarification if necessary.

3. Ask the student to retell all or part of the story.

4. Write what the student says on the board, a piece of paper, or a flip chart page. You could also type it into a computer. If the student makes a mistake, you can correct it. However, try to keep word choices and meaning as close as possible to what the student says.

5. Leave space between lines of writing in case you have to add sentences or make changes later.

6. Read the story aloud to the student. If your student is a beginner, point to each word as you read it. (In this way, you reinforce the connection between spoken and printed words.)

7. Read the story again in a more natural rhythm.

8. Ask if there is anything the student would like to add or change.

9. If the student has some awareness of sound-symbol relationships in English, ask him or her to read each sentence after you read it. Help with any difficult words.

10. Review the story at the next lesson. If possible, type the story and make copies—one for you and one for the student. You can work with him or her to add a title to the story as well.

Topics for LEA Stories

Family

School

Work

Field trips

Vacations (real or imagined)

Problems with health, money, car, or neighbors

Something the student is happy about or proud of

Everyday routines

Descriptions of people

Comparison between American life/culture and life/culture in the student's country

Dreams

Prompts such as "Someday I hope my children will…," "When I was young, I thought…," "If I could have three wishes, they would be…," or "I feel happy when…"

A favorite hobby

The strangest thing that ever happened to the student

SUGGESTIONS

- Use LEA stories to work on a student's reading skills. Some things you can do:

  ▷ Practice sequencing. Using strips of cardstock paper, write one sentence from the story on one cardstock strip. Then cut out the individual words from the sentence so there is only one word to a small card. Mix up the small cards, and ask the student to assemble them into a correct sentence. Or write each sentence on a separate card, and ask the student to put the cards in the correct sequence.

  ▷ Do a cloze exercise (see Activity 31.)

  ▷ See other activities in this chapter for some additional ideas for building skills with LEA stories.

- If you are working with a group, find a topic that they all know something about—for example, a field trip that the class recently took together. Have students take turns adding sentences to the story. Read the completed story to them. Then read the story aloud as a group. Finally, encourage individuals to try reading the story aloud.

- Take your time during this activity. It is important to give beginning-level students lots of time to think so that they can say what they really want to say. Learn to wait silently and patiently while your students consider how to put ideas into words.

- Work with a student to create a semantic web of ideas about a particular topic. (See Activity 44.) The student can then base an LEA story on one of the ideas. Often the ideas generated in one web can serve as the basis for several different stories.

- When working with very beginning readers, keep stories short—only two or three sentences. Read the story aloud with a student before you ask him or her to try to read it alone.

- With beginning readers, base LEA activities on sentence starters. Have the student dictate the rest of the sentence as you write it.

Examples:

I want _____.

I can _____.

My children are _____.

I wish _____.

Building Skills with LEA Stories
(beginning, intermediate)

Activity 26

PURPOSE

To use LEA stories to reinforce reading and writing lessons.

METHOD

You can use LEA stories to teach many different skills. Students are more likely to learn a skill when it is connected to their own words. For example, here are some things students can do with their LEA stories:

- Copy stories into their notebooks for writing practice.

- Circle every *e* (or some other letter) in a story.

- Underline every capital letter.

- Count the number of sentences.

- Make flashcards for words they would like to learn. Ask students to practice with the cards—alone or with someone else—until they can read the words by sight. (See Activity 28.)

- Reconstruct scrambled sentences from the story. In other words, you can write the words from a sentence in the wrong order. Students rearrange the words in the right order.

- Write contractions from the story, and say what words they stand for (e.g., *wasn't/was not*).

- Circle all the adjectives.

- Give a word or phrase that means the opposite of words you underlined in the story (e.g., *tall/short; got married/got divorced*).

- Locate on a map the places mentioned in the story.

- Choose four or five words to learn to spell.

- Identify cause-and-effect relationships ("Why did this happen?").

- Reread the story for fluency.

- Ask yes-or-no or *wh-* questions based on the story.

- For more ideas on how to create stories with students and use them for practice, review the webpage "Using Students' Stories in Lessons," created by the Jones Library, Amherst, Massachusetts. You can find it at **http://www.joneslibrary.org/esl/tutors/stories.html**.

Pre-Reading Activities

Pre-reading activities help provide context for a reading and enable students to connect their background knowledge to that reading:

- They allow students to approach reading with a better understanding of what they are about to read.

- They help students feel prepared.

- They enable students to make valid predictions about the content of the reading.

- They increase the probability that students will be able to figure out an unfamiliar word.

For example, if students know that the reading selection is about automobile safety, they can predict what the words in this sentence might be:

You should wear a _____ _____ when you drive.

- They ensure that all students in a learning group have access to the same basic background knowledge.

Pre-Reading Activity—Discussion (all)

PURPOSE

To use discussion to develop the student's base of knowledge about a specific topic before reading something related to that topic.

METHOD

1. Tell students what topic they will read about in a story.

2. Ask questions about the topic. For example, if the topic is "What to do when you get sick," possible questions might be:

   What do you do when you get sick?

   Why do you go to the doctor?

   What happens when you go to the doctor?

   What is a prescription?

   What is another way to get medication?

SUGGESTIONS

Here are some other ideas for pre-reading activities:

- Use a sentence completion activity to generate discussion. For a reading selection about elections or government, you could ask students to complete the following sentence: "If I were president, I would . . ."

- Ask students to help you construct a semantic web showing what they already know about the topic. (See Activity 44.)

- Read the title of the selection aloud, and ask students to predict what they think it will be about.

- Create an information grid related to the topic, and ask students to help you complete it. (See Activity 50.)

- Set a purpose for the reading by asking students to find the answer to a specific question as they read.

- Select a picture (or more than one picture, if necessary) related to the topic of the reading. Show the picture and ask students to describe what they see happening in the picture or to imagine what the people in the picture are thinking.

Recognizing Words

To understand an author's message, a reader needs to apply his or her own prior knowledge and experience to the topic. This can't happen, however, if the reader is unable to recognize many of the words in the text.

Recognition is the ability to match words in print with words the reader already uses and whose meaning the reader already knows. Good readers are able to draw on one of five word recognition strategies to do this (see box).

No single strategy works for all situations, and sometimes students need to use multiple strategies to figure out a word. The more strategies a person knows, the more likely it is that the person can recognize words successfully. The activities that follow help to teach the strategies. They can be taught in any order. Start by building on what the student already knows.

Word Recognition Strategies

Sight Words

These are words that students recognize instantly without having to stop to figure them out. The more proficient a reader is, the more words he or she recognizes by sight.

Phonics

Students who know sound-symbol relationships can use them to recognize words.

Word Patterns

Recognizing familiar letter groupings can help students figure out words.

Context

Students can use surrounding words to help recognize an unfamiliar word.

Word Parts

Recognizing word roots, prefixes, suffixes, and other word parts can help students understand a word.

Sight Words (beginning)

PURPOSE

To help beginning-level students recognize as many words as possible by sight in order to improve reading speed and comprehension.

METHOD

1. Identify a group of words that a student wants to learn. This may be words used in daily life, words found in Language Experience stories, words that regularly appear in stories from a textbook, words that appear often in general writing (e.g., *the, there, this,* and *was*), or survival words (e.g., words found on road signs or in public places).

2. Show these words to your student. Ask him or her to print the selected words on index cards. (You can help if needed.) Make a set of cards for yourself.

3. If the student has trouble remembering a word, ask him or her to use the new word in a sentence. Write the sentence. Ask the student to copy the sentence on the back of the flashcard. You can also ask students to draw pictures of the words on the backs of their cards.

4. Show each card (from your own set), and ask the student to read it.

5. Encourage students to review their own flashcards at home.

6. Review the words often.

SUGGESTIONS

*   Take time to teach words orally first to ensure that students know the meanings before you teach them as sight words.

*   Teach no more than six to ten new words at a time.

*   Divide the cards into two piles: words that a student knows and those that are still difficult. Work with the student to reduce the size of the second pile.

*   Punch a hole in each card, and bind them together with a key ring.

*   Set a specific amount of time. Ask a student to read as many cards as possible in that time. Repeat the exercise to show improvement.

*   Talk about any new words, or ask students to use the words in sentences. This enables students to develop fuller contexts for words, and that improves oral skills and makes it easier for students to recognize the words in print.

- If a student is keeping a personal dictionary, have him or her add the words to the dictionary.

Activity 29

Phonics—Teaching Consonant Sounds (beginners)

PURPOSE

To enable beginning-level students to decode unfamiliar words by using their knowledge of sound-letter relationships.

METHOD

1. From a reading selection or from a Language Experience story, select two or three words that begin with the same consonant and sound (e.g., *cat, come,* and *car*).

2. Ask students to write each word on a piece of paper and underline the initial consonant.

3. Ask students to name the letter. Teach it if necessary.

4. Say the sound of the letter, and ask students to repeat after you.

5. Ask for examples of other words that start with that sound, or give examples yourself.

6. Write these words down. Say the sound as you underline the letter at the beginning of the word. (Be careful to use only words that start with the same letter *and* have the same sound. For example, you might use *park* and *pig* but not *phone*.)

7. Have students practice identifying the same initial sound in other words that they know.

8. If a student needs help remembering a sound, ask him or her to choose a key word that will help. Examples: *car* for /c/, *hand* for /h/.

SUGGESTIONS

- Use the same technique to teach consonant blends and digraphs.

consonant blend: Two or three consonants that are pronounced almost as one sound. Examples: *pl, str.* You hear the sound of each letter.

digraph: A group of two letters that expresses one sound. Example: *sh.*

- After students can identify consonant sounds at the beginning of words, repeat the process to teach consonant sounds at the end and in the middle of words.

- Review sounds taught in previous lessons.

- For an idea on how to use minimal pairs to help students distinguish between frequently confused vowel or consonant sounds, see Activity 24.

- For additional information on teaching consonant and vowel sounds, see the *Laubach Way to English* series from New Readers Press.

- For assistance in describing individual sounds, see pages 84–85 and Appendix A.

- As you practice sounds and letters more frequently, use this exercise from time to time. When a student does not know how to spell a word, draw a blank on a piece of paper for each letter. Have the student listen to the word and try to guess what letter should be in each blank. Fill in a blank with each correct guess.

Activity
30

Word Patterns (beginning)

PURPOSE

To help students recognize new words more quickly without having to sound out and blend each separate sound in the word.

METHOD

1. Make sure students understand the concept of rhyming. Say several pairs of words, and ask if they rhyme.

2. Choose a word pattern with which you can create several rhyming words, for example, *-it.*

3. Write the word pattern at the top of a piece of paper, and ask a student to say the sound. If no one knows the sound, say it yourself. Example: *-it.*

4. Below the pattern, write a word that ends in that pattern. Example: *sit.* (Throughout the activity, use words the student knows orally.) Ask a student what the word is. Read it yourself if he or she is unsure.

5. Write a word that rhymes with the first word (and has a different initial consonant). Example: *bit.* Ask a student to read it. If he or she has difficulty, give a hint: "If *s-i-t* is *sit,* then what is *b-i-t?*"

TEACHING ADULTS: AN ESL RESOURCE BOOK

6. Keep adding words and asking students to read them.

7. Ask students to add other words using the same pattern. If they have difficulty coming up with words, offer some of your own. Take the time to teach the meaning of the words. Note that a student might create a word that is not a real word in English. If this happens, explain that there is no such word, but compliment the person on his or her understanding of the concepts of patterns and rhyming.

8. Ask students to read through the entire list.

    Example:

    -it
    sit
    bit
    fit
    hit
    lit
    flit

SUGGESTIONS

- Use this recognition strategy to help a student figure out multisyllabic words as he or she tries to identify the pattern in each syllable.

    -ar   **-et**
    tar   get
        target

- Do not confuse beginners by using ending sounds that can be spelled more than one way. Examples: *fix* and *picks, tax* and *stacks.*

- When students are comfortable with a pattern, dictate other words that have the same pattern, and ask students to write them.

- See Appendix G in *Teaching Adults: A Literacy Resource Book* (published by New Readers Press) for examples of common word patterns.

- Make flashcards, one for the pattern and one for each beginning letter. Students can put the pattern card together with each of the other cards to create various new words. Then they can read the new words aloud.

- Fold an index card, and cut a window in one side of it to make a "word slide." Tape the top and bottom of the card together, and write the word ending next to the window. On a separate card, write the beginning letters that you want to work with. A student can pull this card through the word slide and read each new word as the letters appear in the window.

Activity 31

Context—Cloze Procedure (all)

PURPOSE

To help students practice using context—the meaning of surrounding words and sentences—to fill in missing words in a sentence or paragraph. (The word *cloze* comes from *closure* and means finishing or "closing" a sentence.)

METHOD

1. Select a passage that is at or below the student's reading level. Leave the first sentence intact. For beginning readers, delete approximately every tenth word. (You can make this exercise more challenging for a higher-level student by deleting more words, e.g., every fifth word.) The following example deletes every fifth word:

> Every day I went to look in the bird's nest. Yesterday there were four _____ in the nest. The _____ wasn't there. When she _____ back, she quickly hopped _____ the nest and sat _____ the eggs.

2. Have the student read the sentences and fill in the missing words.

SUGGESTIONS

- If you want to make this activity easier, provide a word list so students know which words are missing. Or you can write the first letter of each word on the line to serve as a clue.

- Remind students to choose words that make sense in context. Unless students are working from a word list, there may be more than one right answer.

- Use material with which students are already familiar, such as a Language Experience story or a passage from a previous lesson.

- If the material is new, give students an overview of the contents before they start reading. When you use new material, make sure it relates in some way to content you have introduced before—through, for instance, vocabulary words or topics.

- If a student has difficulty writing, ask him or her to write only the first letter of the word or to say the word while you write it.

- As a follow-up activity, go back and ask students to explain why they selected those particular words.

Word Parts—Compound Words
(high-beginning, intermediate)

PURPOSE

To help students put words together to form compound words.

METHOD

1. Select five or six compound words that are made up of smaller words that students can already read.

2. Write the first part of each word in one column (on a chalkboard or large piece of paper).

3. Write the second part of each word in a second column. Do not put them in the same order as in the first column.

4. Ask a student to draw a line to connect a word in the first column to a word in the second column and form a compound word. Have the student read the new word aloud.

5. If you're not sure a student recognizes a word, ask him or her to use it in a sentence.

6. Give each student a chance to find and read a compound word.

Example:

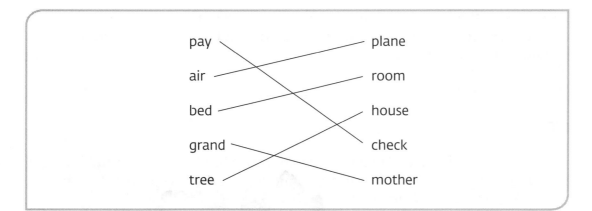

Developing Fluent Oral Reading

Many ESL students who do not read English well are unsure of their reading ability and read haltingly, with little or no expression. This can be the case even if they have already learned the vocabulary words orally. They often pause and wait for the tutor or teacher to tell them how they're doing. Such students need to develop confidence and learn how to read fluently because fluent reading will improve their ability to understand and enjoy what they read. In addition, some students have specific goals that require oral reading, such as reading stories to children or reading religious texts aloud.

Three oral techniques for teaching reading are listed below. These techniques are described later in the chapter. The first provides the most support: The student listens as you read aloud. The next two techniques are designed to increase independence to the point at which the student is reading alone.

Reading to the student: Student listens as tutor reads.

Duet reading: Tutor and student read together.

Echo reading: Tutor reads first and then student reads the same sentence or paragraph.

Activity 33   *Reading Aloud to Students* (beginning)

PURPOSES

To allow students to hear someone read with good expression and phrasing, and to make it possible for students to use materials that are too hard for them to read independently.

To allow the student to practice listening to English that will be somewhat challenging for him or her to understand.

To enable the tutor or teacher to share with the student materials that he or she has found interesting, thus exposing the student to possible new ideas and building the tutor-student relationship.

To provide a change of pace in the lesson.

METHOD

1. Select a short passage or text that you know will be of interest to your students. Make sure they know the meanings of most of the words, but they don't have to be able to read the material.

2. Tell students that you are going to read aloud. Ask them to tell you if they don't understand something as you read.

3. Have students either follow along in a copy of the text or sit next to you and look at your reading selection.

4. Read the passage aloud.

SUGGESTIONS

- You may want to discuss the topic beforehand to ensure that students are capable of understanding most of what you will be reading. Teach any new vocabulary orally.

- It is more important for students to hear you read than for them to follow along word by word in the passage. If a student becomes frustrated over losing the place while trying to follow along, ask him or her to just listen.

- Look for texts geared toward adult students—from textbooks used by your program or elsewhere. Although children's books might have the appropriate language level for your students, you don't want them to feel they are being treated like children. That said, reading a children's book could be a good technique if your students are focused on improving English to help their children at school.

Activity
34

Duet Reading (intermediate, advanced)

PURPOSE

To give fluency practice without putting a student on the spot by asking him or her to read difficult material alone.

Duet reading helps ESL students to do the following:

- Pay attention to punctuation marks.

- Develop good eye movement in order to keep the place.

- Read words in natural phrases.

- Learn new sight words.

- Read with expression.

- Read for enjoyment.

METHOD

Use duet reading after students develop some basic sight vocabulary.

1. **Choose something that is a little too hard for a student.**

   Collect several books, magazine or newspaper articles, pamphlets, or brochures that address topics of interest and that are somewhat above the student's current reading level. Ask him or her to select which piece to read.

2. **Begin reading together.**

   Sit next to the student, and read aloud together from the same selection. Read at a normal speed, using expression and observing punctuation. The student reads along and tries to keep up with you.

3. **Use your finger.**

   Move your finger beneath the line as you read to help the student keep up.

4. **Keep going.**

   Continue to read at a normal rate even if the student hesitates or falls behind. Stop if he or she stops reading completely.

5. **Don't ask questions.**

   Do not ask any questions to check the student's understanding. Do not stop to explain the meaning of a word unless the student asks. This material is to be used only as an oral reading exercise.

6. **Decide whether the reading material is at the right level.**

   If the student keeps up easily, select more challenging material. If the material seems too difficult, find something that may be easier because it is written more simply or because the student knows more about the subject.

SUGGESTIONS

- Use duet reading only for brief periods (seven to ten minutes).

- Don't ask students to read aloud from the material by themselves. The material is above their independent reading level, so that could be a frustrating experience.

- If you use duet reading at the beginning of a lesson, reread part of the same selection with the student at the end of the lesson. Then the student can see how much easier it gets with practice.

- Use this technique to practice fluent reading with a student's own writing or with stories at his or her level.

TEACHING ADULTS: AN ESL RESOURCE BOOK

Activity 35

Echo Reading (all)

PURPOSE

To provide support by first modeling reading a passage and then asking a student to read the same passage aloud independently.

METHOD

1. Select material that is somewhat above a student's independent reading level.

2. Check to make sure the student understands key vocabulary before you begin reading.

3. Read each sentence aloud, and then ask the student to read it aloud.

4. Encourage the student to try reading independently as soon as he or she is comfortable doing so.

SUGGESTIONS

- After you both have read several sentences (or paragraphs), you could ask the student to read the entire section again.

- You can also use this strategy with material at the student's reading level if the student needs help reading fluently.

- Encourage students to use digital recorders or smartphones to record you as you read, so they can practice reading aloud at home. Alternately, you can read aloud passages found online or audio passages that are now commonly part of textbooks (these might include audio CDs or digital downloads). Another option is have students practice with *News for You Online,* an easy-to-read weekly news source that is available by subscription from New Readers Press, **http://www.newreaderspress.com**. All stories are recorded and can be played back either in their entirety or sentence by sentence.

Activity 36

Using the SQ3R Reading Approach (advanced)

PURPOSE

To help ESL students meet two academic goals: to develop note-taking skills and to analyze text.

METHOD

Explain to students that SQ3R is a method for approaching textbook chapters or other types of reading such as newspaper and magazine articles. The method consists of five steps: Survey, Question, Read, Recite/Retell, and Review. It also involves a graphic organizer that students can use. This method helps readers discover important facts and ideas from what they are reading.

The Basic Activity

SURVEY

Tell students that during the Survey step, they should look at the reading's title, introductory and summary paragraphs, and boldface headings. They also should look at all graphics and captions. This survey should take only a few minutes (for example, ten minutes is ideal if the student is surveying a textbook chapter). "The purpose of the survey is to get a general idea about how subtopics are broken down and how much time it will take you to read the chapter," according to the National College Transition Network (**http://www.collegetransition.org**). On their graphic organizer, students can note the reading's title and headings.

QUESTION

Ask students to turn each boldface heading into a question. The questions should use the *wh-* words—*who, what, where, when,* and *why*—and *how.* By doing this, students determine a reason for their reading and can answer these questions as they go along. Students can write the questions they have created under the Question area of their graphic organizer.

READ

Next, students should read the text below each heading to find answers to the questions they wrote in the previous step. Usually this answer will include the main idea as well as some supporting details. Students should highlight or underline only this information. This is also the time for students to reread sections that they find particularly difficult. Students can write answers to the questions they generated in the Read section of their graphic organizer.

RECITE/RETELL

Students should recite answers to their original questions, trying to put answers in their own words and not reading what they wrote on their graphic organizer. "The purpose for doing this is to help think about and understand what you have read. If you rewrite or rephrase what you have read, it aids in comprehension," according to the National College Transition Network. Under the section Recite/Retell on the graphic organizer, students can write in answers to their questions in their own words.

REVIEW

Prompt students to reread their questions and answers. They should then cover their answers and ask themselves—or each other—their questions. As students feel they have mastered a particular question, they can place a check mark beside it. There is no section for Review on the graphic organizer; during this final step, students are reviewing their information from the previous steps.

Tell students that they can use the SQ3R method to read an article (as we have done here) or read a new section of a longer text, such as a section of a textbook chapter.

Election News

Taking a Critical Look at Campaign Ads

The candidate faces the camera. How can we be better off, he asks, "when America is billions in debt, when prices have doubled and taxes break our backs, and we are still fighting (overseas)?"

He shakes his head.

"It's tragic," he says. "And it's time for a change."

Which presidential candidate said this?

It was Dwight D. Eisenhower, in 1952. The Republican war hero ran against Adlai Stevenson. He won on a promise to clean up "the mess in Washington."

The words are from one of Eisenhower's television campaign ads. If the theme sounds familiar, that doesn't surprise David Schwartz.

He says the style and techniques of campaign ads may change over the years. But the basic messages are still the same.

"It's time for a change; you see that message over and over again," he says.

Exhibit Looks at Campaign Ads Over Time

Schwartz knows what he is talking about. He is the chief curator of an online exhibit of presidential campaign ads through TV history.

The exhibit is called "The Living Room Candidate." It is presented by the Museum of the Moving Image in Astoria, New York.

The title refers to the room where most of us see the ads that affect our views of the candidates. Visitors to www .livingroomcandidate.org can watch the ads by year. They can choose ads by issue, such as war or taxes. They can also choose types of ads they want to see. Those might include ads that feature children, fear messages, or a candidate's life story.

Analyzing Ads

The number and speed of today's ads can be overwhelming to voters. Schwartz says that's why the museum exhibit is valuable.

"We're trying to help people be thoughtful about how they watch" the ads, he says. "We want them to be more critical of what they see."

When viewers see an old trick or technique in ads, he says, they can look past that to the real message. They should also check the facts in an ad, he says, by reading news reports and visiting Web sites such as www.factcheck .org. That site is hosted by the Annenberg Foundation.

"The ability to evaluate these ads is crucial," Schwartz says. Votes can be changed by these images.

(Adapted from *News for You*, a weekly publication of New Readers Press. © October 1, 2008. For more information on *News for You*, go to **www.newsforyouonline.com.**)

(Activity adapted from "Using the SQ3R Reading Approach," *Notebook*, Fall 2010, pp. 6–8.)

TOPIC: PRESIDENTIAL CAMPAIGN ADS
(ARTICLE TITLE: TAKING A CRITICAL LOOK AT CAMPAIGN ADS)

Survey	Question	Read	Recite/Retell
1. Exhibit looks at campaign ads over time.	1. What is the exhibit?	1. The exhibit is "The Living Room Candidate." It is an exhibit of presidential campaign ads throughout TV history. Visitors to www.livingroomcandidate.org can watch ads by years. They can also choose ads by issue or choose the types of ads they want to see.	1. This article talks about presidential campaign ads. These kinds of ads are part of an exhibit called "The Living Room Candidate," at a museum in New York. Viewers can pick the ad they want to see by the date it was on TV or by what topic it was about.
2. Exhibit analyzes ads.	2. Why analyze ads?	2. The number and speed of today's ads can be overwhelming to voters. The exhibit is trying to help people be thoughtful about how they watch ads. It is trying to help them evaluate what they see more critically.	2. Those who work at the museum want people to think more about what they see. Viewers need to try to find the real message and not get confused by tricks or techniques in an ad.

Getting Started with Writing

Because some ESL students are unfamiliar with the Roman alphabet, you might have to begin by teaching how to write the letters. In most cases, it is best to start with printing (sometimes called "manuscript writing") rather than with cursive writing.

Activity 37 can be used to teach how to write the letters of the alphabet.

When students can do this comfortably, you can encourage them to copy words and sentences. This will help them learn the proper spacing to use between letters and words, when to use capital letters, and where to place punctuation marks. Asking students to copy all or part of their own Language Experience stories is an excellent way to start.

Here are some other useful activities for developing basic writing skills:

- Make lists (of family members, groceries to buy, chores to do, bills to pay, jobs the student has held).

- Write appointments, birthdays, or other special occasions on a calendar.

- Fill out sample forms (job applications, checks, medical forms).

- Write emails.

- Write entries in an address book.

- Write words on flashcards to learn as sight words.

- Create personal dictionaries of words that students want to remember or use often.

Letter Formation—Five Steps to Printing (beginning)

PURPOSE

To teach printing to students who do not write in any language or who are unfamiliar with the Roman alphabet.

METHOD

1. Select a letter that needs practice; then face the same direction as the students, and demonstrate each stroke needed to print the letter. Make broad strokes in the air (as if you are spray painting on the wall). Describe each stroke as you make it. Then ask the students to move through the strokes with you.

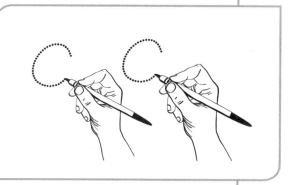

2. Make the letter in large strokes on unlined paper or on a whiteboard/blackboard. Then ask the student to trace over the letter using the same strokes.

3. Write the letter on lined paper. Use paper with three guide lines. Explain that all letters stand on the bottom guide line. Some letters start from the top guide line and some from the middle guide line. Some letters descend below the bottom line. Then print the letter on the guide lines, and ask the student to trace it.

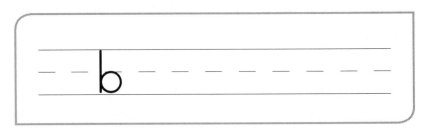

4. Ask the student to use a pencil to practice printing the same letter several times on the guide lines.

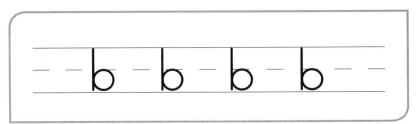

SUGGESTIONS

- If a student is new to printing letters, encourage him or her to use a fat pencil or a pencil grip.

- Remember that students may want to complete the letter practice for homework rather than doing the whole thing in class.

- Teach the letters in alphabetical order, or help a student learn to print the letters in his or her name first.

- Make sure that students have plenty of room on the table and that their chairs and tables are at a comfortable height. Be sure there is enough light as well.

- Provide pencils with erasers. Many students do not like to leave mistakes or have messy papers. Pencils will be easier to use if they have somewhat dull points, because new writers tend to exert a lot of pressure.

- Limit writing practice for beginners to prevent hand fatigue or cramps. Limit the number of new letters you introduce in each lesson. One or two may be enough.

- Keep a chart of the letters and numbers (see pages 115–116) available for reference until students can write all of them independently.

Sample Printing Chart

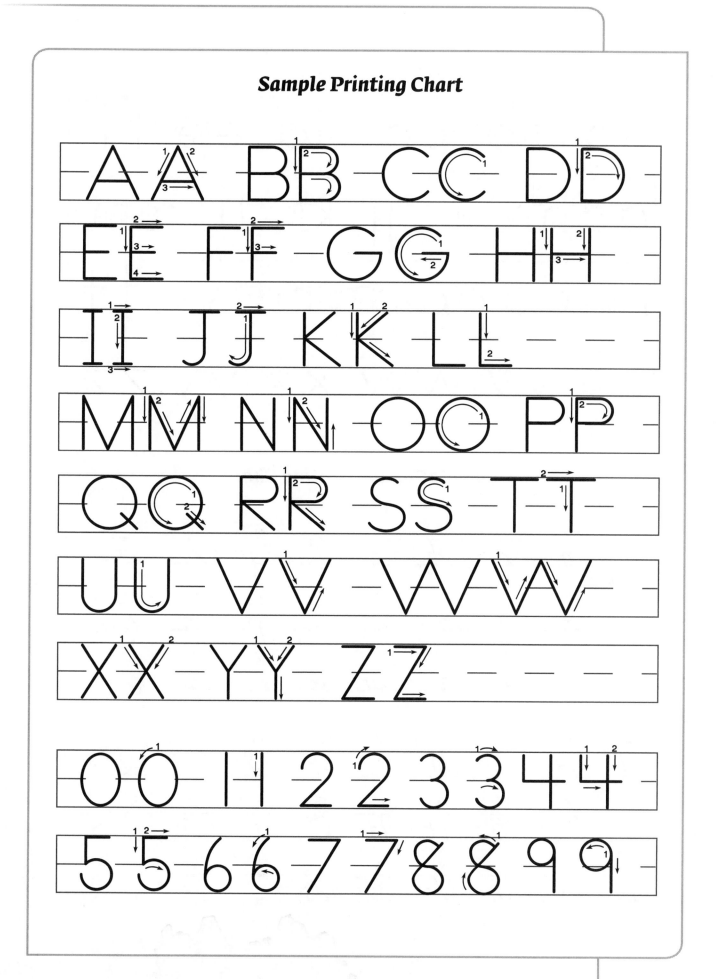

aa bb cc dd ee ff

gg hh ii jj kk ll mm

nn oo pp qq rr ss tt

uu vv ww xx yy zz

Sample Cursive Writing Chart

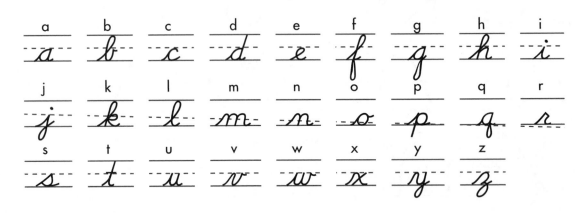

- If a student is having a lot of difficulty remembering the shape of a letter, ask him or her to describe the shape and relate it to a familiar object as a memory "key." Examples: O is round like an orange; J looks like a fishhook.

- Teach students the difference between uppercase and lowercase letters.

- Remember that letters can look very different depending on the typeface used. To help students recognize letters of the alphabet in different typefaces, select examples from magazines and newspapers or from the word processing program on a computer. Cut out these letters from printed material, and paste them on sheets of paper, a separate sheet for each letter. As an alternative, ask students to find and cut out their own examples.

Guided Writing

When ESL students are able to write the letters of the alphabet and copy words and sentences or write them from dictation, they are ready to begin creating their own texts—using writing to share their own ideas and experiences.

At this stage, beginning ESL students often approach writing as a grueling task. They worry about making grammatical mistakes, misspelling words, or writing something that no one will understand. They often view writing as an agonizing act of creating something for the teacher or tutor to correct. As a result, they become overly concerned with the technical aspect of writing—of getting it "right." They lose sight of the fact that writing is a tool for communicating ideas. Because of this, they don't see themselves as writers, and they fail to appreciate all the strengths they bring to the writing process.

As a tutor, your challenge will be to balance encouraging your students' successful communication in writing with correcting obvious errors that would impede such communication.

Activities in this chapter help students to begin writing sentences. Others share ideas for encouraging students to write independently and do free writing. The initial activities all involve "guided writing." *You* decide the topic and develop a controlled structure that allows students to express their ideas without having to struggle unnecessarily. Free writing activities give students more leeway to choose topics and express themselves.

Collaborative writing is especially useful with multilevel groups. Each student contributes at his or her ability level, and all share equally in the success of the final product. A student who has never written more than a sentence or two can still feel proud of having made an important contribution to a much longer piece of writing.

Because group members share the responsibility for the task, the stress that often accompanies writing lessons is greatly reduced in collaborative writing. Students are free to focus on what they're saying, and to enjoy the creative process. They will find their own ideas stimulated by reading and hearing the ideas of others in the group. Finally, the fun and creativity that develop during collaborative activities often carry over to other writing tasks and help make students more willing to tackle writing in general.

Activity
38
Sentence Completion with Pictures (all)

PURPOSE

To help students complete sentences and generate sentences of their own after they have looked at picture stimuli.

METHOD

1. Select a picture or photograph. The picture should depict vocabulary that the students know. For example, if students have recently learned color names or names of clothing items, the picture might feature various people in a city wearing different types of colorful clothing.

2. Tell students that this is a writing activity. Explain that you will start to say sentences about the picture and they will complete the sentences. You can make the sentence frames as easy or as difficult as you feel is appropriate. Read the sentence frames aloud to the students. Here are some examples:

> The man is _____.
>
> The tree is big and _____.
>
> The woman looks very _____.
>
> The policeman is trying to _____.
>
> No one is noticing that _____.

3. Ask a student to read each completed sentence.

Activity 39

Using Pictures in One-to-One Tutoring
(beginning)

PURPOSE

To support beginning students as they write original sentences in response to questions about pictures.

METHOD

1. Show students a picture, photograph, or drawing depicting one person. Some possible ideas for pictures:

   • A picture of the student (so he or she will write about himself or herself)

   • A picture of a friend or family member

   • A picture of someone in a magazine or newspaper

2. Ask the student to think about the person in the picture.

3. Ask a question about the picture. ("What's the person's name?") If you are using a picture of a stranger, explain that there are no "right" answers to the questions you will be asking in this activity. The student can make up any answer, but the answer must be in a complete sentence. Have the student answer orally. ("Her name is Anna.")

4. Give the student a piece of paper, and tell him or her to write the answer. Explain that he or she need not be concerned about correct spelling or grammar at this point.

5. Ask a second question that builds on the student's first answer. ("Where does Anna live?") Ask for an oral answer (in a complete sentence).

6. Tell the student to write the answer below the answer to the first question.

7. Continue asking questions, each built on the student's previous response. (You might have to look at his or her paper to see what the previous response was.) Here is an example of how such a guided writing activity might proceed:

Tutor	Student
What's the person's name?	Her name is Anna.
Where does Anna live?	She lives in Los Angeles.
Who does she live with?	She lives with her mother, father, and two sisters.
How old is she?	She is 18 years old.
How does she feel about her life?	She is very happy.
Why is she happy?	She's happy because she won $200,000 in the lottery.
What is she going to do with all that money?	She is going to buy a new house, and she will go to college.
Why does she want to go to college?	She wants to be a lawyer.

Here is an example of something a student might write about a picture of himself:

My name is Anh Dung. I am from Vietnam. I am 56 years old. I live in Los Angeles.

8. Ask the student to read aloud the sentences he or she wrote.

SUGGESTIONS

- It is important to avoid questions that can be answered with a yes-or-no response. Otherwise, the student might end up with a story that reads as follows:

Tutor	Student
What's the person's name?	Her name is Anna.
Does Anna live in the country?	No.
Does she live in a city?	Yes.
What city does she live in?	She lives in Los Angeles.

- It is important to have the student form complete sentences so that the story will read like a real story (e.g., "She is 18 years old," not "18 years old").

- If you are teaching a small group, students can take turns reading each other's sentences. They can also take turns writing sentences about pictures of each other.

(Adapted from a presentation given by Sharron Bassano.)

Activity 40
Using Pictures with Small Groups
(intermediate, advanced)

PURPOSE

To enable students to practice writing fluency in a small-group setting.

METHOD

This activity works best with a small group of five or six students. The directions below are for a group of five.

1. Collect five different magazine or newspaper pictures that depict just one person. Each person in the group will need a different picture. (If you are working with several groups, you can use multiple copies of one picture as long as you don't give the same picture to people in the same group.)

2. Give each student a picture with a blank sheet of paper taped or stapled to the back of it.

3. Ask the students to look at their pictures and imagine who the person is and what the person's background and life are like.

4. Write the first set of questions on a board where each member of the group can see them. Read the questions aloud. Example:

What is his/her name?

How old is he/she?

What does he/she do?

5. Ask the students to turn their pictures over and write the answers to these questions (using complete sentences) on the attached piece of paper. Tell them not to worry about correct spelling or grammar. Encourage them to be as imaginative about the person in the picture as they want to be.

6. When they have finished writing, have them pass the picture to the person on the right. (The activity will be easier if the students are seated in a circle or around a table.)

7. Ask each student to look at the new picture, turn it over, and read the sentences written by the previous student.

8. Write the following set of questions on the board. Read them aloud.

> Where does he/she live?
>
> Who does he/she live with?

9. Ask the students to write the answers to these questions on the sheet of paper they are now holding. Remind them that they are writing about the person in the new picture and that they can be as creative as they want to be in their answers.

10. When they finish writing, ask each student to again pass the picture to the right. Repeat steps 7–9 for each of the following questions or sets of questions.

> What does he/she like to do?
> What doesn't he/she like to do?
>
> What did he/she do yesterday? Why?
>
> What is he/she going to do tomorrow?

11. When the students have answered all the questions, ask each person to pass the picture to the right one more time. Everyone should have his/her original picture plus a story containing segments written by each member of the group. The resulting stories are usually quite entertaining.

12. At this point, have the students hold up their pictures and read "their" stories to the other members of their group.

SUGGESTIONS

- If you are working with groups smaller than five, you can either set up a shorter writing task (fewer sets of questions) or instruct students to keep passing their pictures around until the task is finished—even though they will then be working on some of the stories twice.

- If you have to work with larger groups, simply "add to the plot" by providing additional sets of questions.

- Allow enough time for students to look at each new picture and to read the previously written sentences.

- Although everyone in the group contributed equally to each of the stories, the person who started the picture story usually feels some "ownership" for that story, so it's best if the story winds up back with that person at the end.

- You can design questions in a way that encourages students to write about a specific topic the group is studying. Examples: choosing among occupations, going to the doctor or dealing with some other health issue, shopping, or moving into a new apartment or house. This also gives students practice with life skills–related tasks and vocabulary.

- You can simplify this activity for beginning-level students by providing sentence frames for them to complete. With this added control, they will feel more comfortable and be better able to focus on their contribution to the story. You can write the sentence frames on the board for students to copy, or you can make photocopies and attach one set to the back of each picture. Examples of sentence frames:

---

1. This is _____.

   He is _____ years old.

   He lives in _____ with _____.

2. He likes _____, but he doesn't like

   _____.

3. Yesterday he _____ because

   _____.

4. He used to be _____, but now he is

   _____.

5. Tomorrow he will _____.

(Adapted from a presentation by Louis Spaventa.)

Activity 41

Getting and Giving Health Information (all)

PURPOSE

To prepare for a trip to the doctor.

METHOD

1. Copy the form on the following page.

2. Tell the student that he or she will fill out medical information that will help during visits to the doctor. Pre-teach new words. These may include "Primary Medical Conditions," "Allergies," and "Contacts." This is private information, and your student may be uncomfortable working closely with anyone else on it. Be thoughtful about how students may react to the activity, and provide alternatives if necessary.

3. Help the student fill out the form. If he or she is at a beginning level, you may want to break the form-filling part into two sessions.

4. Encourage the student to take the form to medical appointments. Alternately, if students fill out this information at the website **http://medids.com/free-id.php** (or if you help them do so), the website will generate a free medical ID card. Make sure you have access to a printer and paper.

(Adapted from "Getting and Giving Your Health Information," *Notebook,* Winter 2010, pp. 10–13. ProLiteracy.)

Activity 42

Using Craigslist to Sell Goods and Services (intermediate, advanced)

PURPOSE

To help students sell items or job-related services on Craigslist (**http://www.craigslist.org**).

METHOD

Like many of us, students often have personal items they no longer need. Additionally, some adult education students have their own businesses that they want to market inexpensively. Since Craigslist started in 1995, it has become a

Emergency Information

Your Basic Information

First Name _____

Middle Name _____

Last Name _____

Date of Birth (mm/dd/yyyy) _____

Street Address _____

City _____

State _____ Zip Code _____

Home Phone _____

Cell Phone _____

Email Address _____

Physician Information

(Your family doctor)

First Name _____

Last Name _____

Phone Number _____

Physician #2

(Other doctor you see, if any)

First Name _____

Last Name _____

Phone Number _____

Blood Type

_____

Emergency Contacts

(A relative or friend who can help if you have a problem/You will list two people and their contact information.)

First Name _____

Last Name _____

Phone Number _____

2nd Phone _____

Relationship (How is the person related to you?)

_____

First Name _____

Last Name _____

Phone Number _____

2nd Phone _____

Relationship _____

Primary Medical Conditions

(Long-term health problems you have, such as asthma or diabetes)

_____

_____

_____

Known Allergies

(Allergies to food, drugs, plants, animals, etc.)

_____

_____

_____

Current Medications

(Drugs you are taking now/How much? How often?)

Drug Name	Dosage	Frequency

From MedIDs.com. Adapted with permission.

popular website for buying and selling products and services, with 30 billion page views and 50 million new classified ads posted every month. Craigslist reaches 700 geographical areas in 70 countries (**http://www.craigslist.org/about/factsheet**).

Although some precautions are recommended when using Craigslist, the site can be a great tool to help advanced ESL students advertise items or job-related services. The directions assume that the students and you, the tutor or teacher, have some previous experience using computers, so the technology-related prompts encountered in this activity should not be overwhelming. The students must also have email addresses, because Craigslist will email ads to them for confirmation and will notify them when someone is interested in their items or services.

Although not all students will have something they want to sell or advertise, the experience of writing an ad (even if it is not posted) provides useful computer experience as well as practice with succinct writing.

1. Prepare for this lesson by visiting Craigslist in advance to review the kinds of ads that are typically posted under "For Sale" and "Services."

   These are the two sections that you will use with your students. Identify two or three succinct, well-written ads in each area to show them. Also decide on the geographical area where your students will post ads. For some users, there will only be one logical choice, but users in larger metro areas may need to choose from several zones.

   Before your tutoring session, practice opening an account on Craigslist (it's free) so you can better guide them through this part of the activity. You are not required to open an account to sell items, but you do need an account for job/ service-related postings. You can create a sample ad, and Craigslist will email the ad to you for verification before posting it.

2. Ask students if they have experience selling unneeded items.

   They may mention traditional approaches such as having garage sales, selling to friends, or even donating items to charitable organizations. Ask students what they know about selling items online. Possible questions you can ask: "Why might selling online be more effective than traditional approaches? What problems or limitations might arise with this approach?"

   If a student has a business- or job-related service, ask if he or she does any regular advertising for it. This could be the case for someone who operates a business, someone who does babysitting, or someone who is looking for part-time work.

3. Ask students what they know about Craigslist (if anything).

   Explain that it is a popular website for selling items and services as well as for searching for jobs and housing. Tell students that they will each create a Craigslist ad to sell an item they no longer want or to advertise job-related services.

If students don't have anything to sell, encourage each to identify a household item they can write about for practice.

Show students some sample Craigslist ads that you have identified. You can also show them the ads below (these are slightly adapted versions of actual ads that appeared on Craigslist). Ask why these sample ads are effective. Point out their short but useful titles and concise descriptions that show readers why their products or services are unique. The painter ad lists some marketing points on separate lines, making the ad easy to read.

SAMPLE TEXT FOR SELLING AN ITEM

Beautiful Wood Baby Cradle

Rocking baby cradle in very good condition. Light wood tone. Mattress is included. Nice design on each end.

SAMPLE TEXT FOR SELLING A JOB-RELATED SERVICE

Professional Painter/Handyman Available

We can do it all—handyman work, remodeling, painting, pressure washing, and roof repair. Call for a free estimate. Great references available. Licensed and insured. Professional results.
Commercial/residential
Interior/exterior
Drywall and stucco repairs
Roof leaks/roof repair
Call Joe's Precision Painting at 505-555-1212 or email affordablejonesvillepainter@craigslist.org

---

You can mention that including a photo with an ad is an additional way to help sell an item. If someone has a website for a job-related service, he or she may also wish to include that website address in the ad. Students should also know that all ads enable readers to email the person posting the ad directly, which is why not all ads provide phone numbers.

4. Introduce the idea of online selling before the day you actually write the ads. This gives students time to think about what they want to advertise and take pictures if necessary. Tell them to come to the next class ready to advertise an item or job service. If a student has access to a digital camera (or has a camera phone), he or she can take pictures of the item that will be for sale and then send those pictures to his or her email account.

Students can use this worksheet to prepare drafts of their ads.

Worksheet: Craigslist Ad for Selling an Item

YOUR AD TITLE (Clearly identify what you are selling. Include the brand name if available.)

_____

PRICE (Consider how long you have had the item, how much you paid for it originally, and the item's condition. You can search Craigslist for similar items to compare prices. You don't want to charge a price that is much higher or lower than what others on the site are charging.)

$_____

YOUR AD (Craigslist readers should already know from your ad title what you are selling. Use your ad to tell them three or four benefits of the item and to describe its condition.)

_____
_____
_____
_____
_____

Worksheet: Craigslist Ad for Selling a Job-Related Service

YOUR AD TITLE (Clearly identify what your job-related service is, adding one or two adjectives to distinguish you from those advertising similar work.)

_____

YOUR AD (Craigslist readers should already know from your ad title what job service you are offering. Use your ad to tell them three or four benefits of using your job service, such as the kinds or quality of work you do, how competitive your pricing is, the years of experience you have doing this work, and what licenses and/or related insurance you have, if applicable.)

_____
_____
_____
_____
_____
_____
_____
_____

5. Review a student's ad. Provide feedback on ways to make the ad stronger. Consider word choice, ad length, and even layout (e.g., using bullet points instead of continuous lines of text). The student can take note of suggested changes and revise the ads accordingly. Then he or she can decide whether to actually post the ad.

Activity
43

Li's Daily Routine (beginning)

PURPOSE

To encourage students to write and talk about their daily routines.

METHOD

1. Show students the picture story "Li's Daily Routine" below. Explain that a routine is a set of tasks or activities that people complete every day. Have students look at the pictures and tell you what Li and her children do every day. Encourage students to come up with their own explanations for the pictures. There are no right or wrong answers, but you can help as needed with vocabulary, pronunciation, or phrasing.

2. Help students to construct a sentence about each picture. The sentences can begin, "Every morning, Li…" or "At (time), Li…". If students make errors in phrasing sentences, suggest improvements.

3. Have students put the sentences together in a paragraph that begins, "Every morning, Li…".

4. Once a student has completed the paragraph, have him or her read the paragraph to you. Make revisions as needed.

(Adapted from an activity from Lynne Weintraub.)

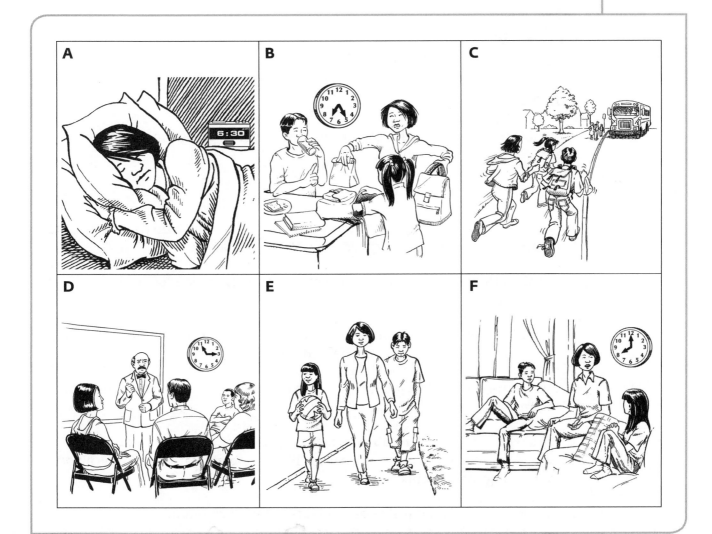

Free Writing

As students get ready for more independent or "free" writing, they may still need help developing their ideas or organizing their thoughts. Activities 44 and 45 represent two ways to help students decide what they want to write about. At this more advanced stage, it's still important to focus on meaning and on effective communication. However, correction of major grammar, spelling, and style errors should also be part of your lessons. Both of these activities are designed to "prime the pump"—to enable students at all levels to get their ideas on paper before they begin to write.

The remaining activities in this section encourage students to be more creative and take greater responsibility for deciding what they want to write and how. This is the time to help students realize that good writers seldom create a finished piece on their first try; they often do a first rough draft and then several revisions as they try to make their ideas clear and complete.

Activity 44

Semantic Webs (all)

PURPOSE

To enable writers to organize their thoughts about a topic before they begin to write.

METHOD

1. Tell students you are going to show something that will help them get started with writing—something called a "web" or a "mind map."

2. Explain that they will first help *you* make a web. Later, students will have a chance to make their own.

3. Tell students that you want to write something about riding in a car. You have lots of ideas but do not know where to start.

4. Write the words *driving in a car* in a circle in the middle of a piece of paper or a board.

5. Ask what students think about when they think of driving in a car (if they don't drive, they can think of what it's like to ride in a car). Develop a semantic web using the students' ideas.

6. When the web is complete, ask students to pick portions of the web and use those to make up some sentences about driving in a car. Provide help as necessary.

Examples of things they might say:
  "There is a lot of traffic when I am driving."
  "I read road signs."
  "I put gas in my car once a week."

7. Write the sentences in the sequence that the students say them. Do not be concerned if the sentences don't seem to relate to each other. Point out any errors in the students' sentences.

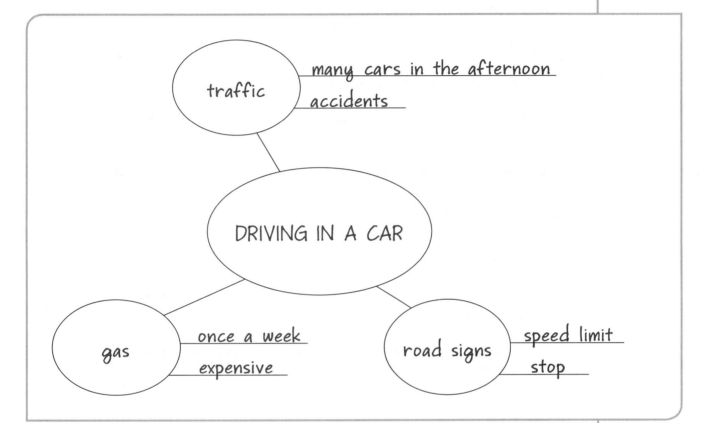

SUGGESTIONS

- During your initial demonstration, you will have to help students draw connections and see possible subtopics. As they see the relationships, they may decide to add more examples.

- You can help students who are struggling with the English words they need to express their ideas. Be prepared to stop and teach any new vocabulary that comes up.

- You can vary the activity by using two webs to generate sentences that compare and contrast. For example, you might want students to write a report about a field trip you took together. You can make the task easier by asking them to first create two webs: "What I liked" and "What I did not like."

Activity 45
Five-Minute Warm-Up (intermediate, advanced)

PURPOSE

To provide an unstructured opportunity for students to capture ideas through sustained writing in preparation for creating a first draft.

METHOD

1. Ask students to take out a pen and several sheets of paper.

2. Work with one or more students to select a topic, or pick a topic that you think would be of interest.

3. Give students five minutes to write everything they know about this topic.

4. Emphasize that they don't have to write complete sentences, nor should they worry about correct grammar, spelling, or punctuation. No one else will read what is written. Later, each student will use this writing to create a first draft about something related to this topic.

5. Encourage students to write whatever pops into their heads and not spend a lot of time thinking about it. Just keep writing!

6. After the five minutes are up, ask each student to read over what he or she has written.

Activity 46
"I Like to Eat Chocolate" (intermediate, advanced)

PURPOSE

To help students understand how to write paragraphs.

METHOD

1. On a sheet of paper, list the numbers 1–10 down the left-hand side. Next to each number, write the same sentence:

I like _____ because _____.

TEACHING ADULTS: AN ESL RESOURCE BOOK

2. Give a copy of this paper to each student.

3. Ask students to try to complete all ten sentences, listing different things that they like and why. Give examples such as:

> "I like pumpkin pie because it tastes sweet."
> "I like to listen to music because it relaxes me."

4. Tell students not to be concerned about getting the grammar, spelling, or punctuation right. They can work on these things later. For now, they should simply enjoy the creative process.

5. After a student has completed some or all of the sentences (completing them all is not important), ask him or her to share the sentences with you.

6. Explain that you would like each student to select one of his or her own sentences and write a paragraph based on that sentence.

7. Share the following definition of a paragraph:

> A paragraph is a group of sentences that are put together because all the sentences are about one topic.

8. Write the following sentence, or use one of the sentences written by a student.

> I like to eat chocolate because it tastes great.

9. Explain that this will be the topic sentence for the sample paragraph. Write this definition:

> A topic sentence indicates what the rest of the paragraph will be about.

10. Explain that the other sentences in the paragraph will give reasons, explanations, or further details about the topic sentence.

11. Show how this works by working together to develop a paragraph based on the sentence you wrote. Encourage the student to help you by suggesting additional sentences.

12. After you have a few sentences, read the paragraph.

13. At this point, do some initial revising as a model for the student. For example, you might add or delete a word or two or rearrange the sentences so they are in a more logical order. Point out any major mistakes that you think could distract from meaning.

14. Ask students to select one of their own sentences and write a short paragraph that starts with that sentence. Tell them to write whatever they want. (Students might provide more information about why they like something or develop a funny story.)

SUGGESTION

- For additional practice, ask students to write another paragraph starting with a different sentence.

(Idea courtesy of Tana Reiff.)

Activity 47 *Writing with Partners* (intermediate, advanced)

PURPOSES

To help students develop a sense of "audience"—who they are writing for.

To provide practice in giving feedback about another person's writing.

To help students use another person's feedback when deciding how to revise their own writing.

To practice working on writing with a partner in a small-group setting.

METHOD

Introduce the activity

1. Tell students you want to show them a way to write on a specific topic. This may be a new way for them to write. Tell them this is meant to be an enjoyable experience. They should relax and have fun.

134

Select a topic

2. Tell the students to pick any topic they'd like to write about. (The first time you do this activity, you may want to have all of the students write on the same topic.)

Develop a shared knowledge base

3. Use this step only if you have required all students to write on the same topic. If so, lead a group discussion on the topic as a pre-writing activity to ensure that everyone has an adequate knowledge base from which to write.

Begin writing

4. Ask students to begin writing on the topic. Tell them not to be concerned at this point with grammar, spelling, word choice, punctuation, how it sounds, or who will read it. Explain that they should concentrate on getting their ideas down on paper.

5. If you are doing this activity for the first time, model step 4 for students. Ask them to watch while you begin to write. Pick a different topic, and use a blackboard or whiteboard, overhead transparency, or projector and LCD screen so everyone can see. Write freely and put your thoughts down as they come into your mind. Again, don't be concerned with correct grammar, spelling, or anything else except the process of writing down your thoughts. Don't correct anything as you go.

Create a first draft

6. Tell the students to think of a close friend or relative.

7. Ask them to write a letter to this person explaining or describing something about the topic. They can choose any aspect of the topic. Remind them again to write freely and not be concerned with correctness. If you have access to a computer lab and feel comfortable with computers, you could have the group write their drafts on the computer.

Share your work

8. Tell the students that you will ask each of them to work with a partner to help them improve what they have written.

9. Explain that you will begin by reading aloud a sample of your own writing. (This should be short—one page or less.) Explain that the students should

   - listen as you read.

   - make a praise statement after you finish reading, saying one good thing about the writing.

   - ask one or two questions that they want you to answer either to clarify something they didn't understand or to ask for more information on the topic.

10. Model this process for the students:

    - Read your piece to them.

    - When you finish, ask for a volunteer to make a praise statement.

    - Then ask other volunteers for questions. Answer their questions.

11. Put students in pairs.

12. Tell them to take turns reading their letters slowly to each other. After the first person finishes reading, the partner makes a praise statement and asks one or two questions (for either clarification or more information). After the reader answers the questions, both students should feel free to further discuss what the first person wrote.

13. Give a signal for the pair to change roles and for the second person to read his or her letter. Repeat step 12.

Revise the writing

14. Ask students to think about their discussions, decide what they'd like to change in their letters based on these discussions, and then rewrite the letters to incorporate these changes.

Edit the writing

15. When students are satisfied with their revisions, work with them to begin editing the pieces—or making them "correct." When you start this process, ask them to focus on only one thing at a time. For example, if you have worked in class on capital letters, you can ask them to check their work to make sure that every sentence begins with a capital letter.

SUGGESTIONS

- If the students are having difficulty picking a topic, offer a short list of topics for them to select from, or ask them questions to stimulate their own thinking.

    Examples:

    "What did you do last weekend?"
    "What do like most about your job?"
    "What is your favorite sport?"

- Use this activity as a follow-up to something the students have done together: reading a story or a newspaper article, or taking a field trip, for example.

- As students become more comfortable with the writing process, give them several opportunities to rethink and revise their writing—just as experienced writers do.

(Adapted from a presentation by Beverly Ann Chin.)

Activity 48 — Adding Sensory Details to Autobiographical Writing (intermediate, advanced)

PURPOSE

To encourage students to add more sensory details to their writing by producing autobiographical pieces. (Getting students to write about themselves is a good way to promote writing.)

METHOD

1. Share the following two writing samples. Read both samples aloud.

Sample 1:
The big dog growled and started chasing me. I ran as fast as I could.

Sample 2:
The big dog showed his yellow fangs, snarled deep in his chest, and raced toward me. As I fled, I heard his snapping jaws and pounding feet behind me, gaining every second.

Ask: "Which writing makes you feel the writer's fear? Why?"

What examples of sensory details—sights, sounds, smells, tastes, or textures—are in these writing samples? Underline those examples and discuss them. Explain that sensory details are important in writing because they attract the reader's attention and make the writing unique. If you have other examples of writings that use good sensory details, show them to the students. Have them identify the sensory details.

2. To give your students practice writing with sensory details, work together to complete the following mind-mapping exercise:

    a. Ask each student to think of a food but not to tell you what the food is. He or she should write the name of the food in the center of a piece of paper and draw a circle around it (but not show you the paper yet).

b. To one side of the food circle, ask the student to write the word *ingredients* and draw a circle around it. Ask the student to draw a line to connect the new circle with the circle around the name of the food. Ask the student to think of the ingredients in that food and to write the ingredients in small subcircles around the ingredients circle.

c. Have the student add circles to describe what the food looks, smells, feels, sounds, and tastes like. For additional practice, students can do circles with steps for how to prepare the food or reasons why the food is or is not good for you.

d. Ask each student to write a paragraph describing his or her food without naming it. Have the students read their paragraphs while you try to guess the food. The description should be strong enough for you to guess correctly.

e. For additional practice, bring food that lends itself easily to sensory description to your class or tutoring session (e.g., an orange, a spice, a colorful doughnut). Brainstorm what that food looks, smells, feels, sounds, and tastes like.

3. Tell your students that each of them will choose one life experience to write about and will focus on using sensory details effectively. The event should be something memorable—something particularly emotional, shocking, or out of the ordinary. Encourage students to think of both big and small events—for example, someone's story of coming to the United States could be a good topic, but one interesting incident that occurred during that journey could just as easily be the focus. Work together to brainstorm ideas.

4. Now have students begin to work on their stories. Ask them to consider the main events of the story and what happened first, second, third, fourth, and fifth. Use the handout on the next page called "Get Ready to Write" to write the main events in the boxes.

5. Ask students to consider what they saw, heard, smelled, tasted, and touched as their events occurred. Those details can be written in the second set of boxes on the next page.

6. Prompt students to number each sensory detail from step 5 according to where it fits in the story. For example, if the smell of oranges hung in the air during the event described in main event box 2, the student should put a number 2 beside that sensory detail.

7. Remind your students of words that can help them move from one event in a story to the next. Put these words on the board, or have them ready on a handout: *first, next, then, later, during, before, soon, until, when, as soon as,* and *meanwhile*.

8. Prompt your students to begin writing, focusing on one main event in each paragraph. Have them insert sensory details where necessary and add transition words, such as those mentioned in step 7.

Get Ready to Write

Consider the main events of your story. What happened first, second, third, fourth, and fifth? Write each main event in the boxes.

1.

▼

2.

▼

3.

▼

4.

▼

5.

What did you see, hear, smell, taste, and touch during your story? Write what you remember in the boxes below. Which event above does each item relate to? Write the number of the event next to each item.

Sights	Sounds	Smells	Tastes	Textures

9. Ask students to review their stories using the rubric below. They can circle whether the story fits the Well Done!, OK, or Needs Work category according to Audience, Structure, Content, Organization, and Word Choice. You can use the rubric to review the story with each student as well. Provide feedback on the following:

- Is the sequence of events clear? Should anything be reordered?

- Does the writing include enough sensory details?

- Can you think of any words that would describe things in a stronger way?

Feature	Well Done!	OK	Needs Work
Audience	Story is written to appeal to its audience.	It is not clear for which audience the story is written.	Story is inappropriate for its audience.
Structure	Well-structured story has a clear beginning, middle, and ending.	Opening does not grab reader's attention. Ending feels incomplete.	Events have no clear beginning or ending.
Content	Story is full of specific sensory details that bring the experience to life.	The writer includes many details, but they don't convey emotional content.	The story has few details; those it does have do not engage the reader.
Organization	Story moves smoothly from an interesting beginning to an engaging middle to a satisfying end.	Sometimes it is hard to follow time sequence.	Story does not flow. Time sequence seems to jump around.
Word Choice	The story uses specific nouns, verbs, and colorful adjectives.	The story uses common, general, and less interesting words.	Vague, overused words make the story seem boring.

(From *Writing Well: Write, Revise, Succeed!* by Libby Wilson. © 2006 New Readers Press. Used with permission.)

10. Ask students to revise their writing, taking account of the feedback.

11. Encourage students to make editing changes to check for spelling, grammar, and word choice.

12. Have students prepare final copies of their writing. For additional expansion, they can illustrate their stories, give them as gifts, or publish them online (there are websites where ESL students can post their writing).

(Adapted from "Adding Sensory Detail to Autobiographical Writing," *Notebook*, Fall 2011, pp. 9–13. The *Notebook* article was adapted from *Writing Well: Write, Revise, Succeed!* by Libby Wilson. 2006. New Readers Press.)

Activity 49 *Dialogue Journals* (intermediate, advanced)

PURPOSE

To give students an opportunity to use and appreciate writing as a form of communication; to correspond with another person in written English.

METHOD

1. Ask each student to bring a notebook to the next class.

2. In the class session, ask each student to write something for you to read in his or her notebook. Tell them that they can choose the topic. For example, students can explain something to you, ask you a question, tell a joke, tell you what they did last weekend, describe a fond memory—anything.

3. Tell students not to worry whether their grammar or spelling is correct or whether any wording sounds funny. The important thing is writing something that they want to write and want to share with *you*.

    By not having to focus on correctness, students can begin—often for the first time—to appreciate writing as a way to communicate their ideas to someone else and not just as another exercise that they have to do. This may encourage them to use writing to meet their daily communication needs outside of class.

4. Explain that you will not correct or change anything they write and that the writing will be confidential. No one except you will see it. You can review the writing as soon as they finish. Tell your students that this is the first of many written exchanges you will have in the form of a dialogue journal. Tell students that the next time they write in their journals, they will do it at home.

5. Give students time to do the writing. If a student is having difficulty getting started, talk with him or her and ask questions. For example, you could suggest that the student write about what he or she did the previous weekend.

6. When you've read a journal entry, put the current date below the student's entry and write your response. If the student asked questions, try to answer them. If not, make comments triggered by what the student wrote. By responding to what students write, you will help them understand that their ideas are worthwhile and meaningful. You will also help them gain a better sense of how to write for a specific audience—you!

7. Although you will not make any corrections to a student's entry, model correct English in what you choose to write yourself. For example:

December 1

Wishing to go home Cristmas,

December 5

I wish I could go home for Christmas, too.

I haven't been home for Christmas in three years. When was the last time you were home?

8. Since your goal is to keep the dialogue going, consider ending each of your entries with a question. This can make it easier for a student to get started on a new entry. But explain to your students that they don't have to limit themselves to answering your questions. They can also choose to write about an entirely different topic.

9. Continue this process through subsequent weeks, except have students take their journals home and write in them there. (Alternately, all of the writing could take place via email or in a word processing program, and students could email you their entries.) Students will write during class only in the session in which you first introduce dialogue journals. You might want to require one entry from each student each week. You'll probably find that students are initially reluctant to do much writing: They will still be trying to figure out what the assignment "really" is. Eventually, a true dialogue will develop.

SUGGESTIONS

-   Use printing when you write in the journals—especially when you are working with beginning students. If you are corresponding by email, then handwriting is not an issue.

-   Be patient. With time, students will become more communicative, and their writing will be more varied, complex, and creative.

-   Remember that dialogue journals are not meant to replace other writing activities you do with students. They do, however, provide an enjoyable alternative to more traditional writing exercises.

-   Although the focus of dialogue journals is free writing without corrections, it's OK to correct a student's writing if he or she asks you to do so.

TEACHING ADULTS: AN ESL RESOURCE BOOK

Integrated Communication Activities

Some of the most effective ESL teaching activities encourage students to communicate with others to complete a task. Integrated communication activities involve all four basic language skills: listening, speaking, reading, and writing. Students work with the tutor or teacher or, in a group setting, with each other on a task that requires them to think critically and to use their language skills. The focus is on the task at hand, not on the skills themselves.

Although the integrated communication activities described in this chapter are designed for beginning-level students, they can be adapted for more advanced students as well. In any case, students need to have some facility in all four basic language skills to take part in the activities.

If you work in a one-to-one situation as a tutor, you may want to consider how you can still use these valuable practice opportunities. For example, can you enlist the help of a volunteer or two for these activities? Activity 53 includes some specific ways to adapt integrated communication activities such as information grids into a one-to-one situation.

Information Grids

An information grid activity is interactive. It involves students in purposeful classroom communication that they can apply to practical tasks in the outside world. The grid itself is a learning aid in table form created by the tutor or teacher. The grid helps students organize information on a specific topic.

Information grids are typically created around topics related to the students' backgrounds and interests. One of the most common topics is personal information about the students themselves. Students will need to provide this kind of information when applying for jobs, enrolling their children in school, or seeking medical assistance. In such situations, people are often required to enter this information on specific forms. Such forms seldom allow people to give answers in complete sentences as students might have been practicing in class.

For example, a job application form usually requires the applicant to briefly list previous jobs, employers, and reasons for leaving those jobs.

Information grids provide effective practice in listening and speaking. Students answer the tutor's questions and ask each other questions. They also have the opportunity to practice their reading, writing, and critical thinking skills as they work together to complete the grids.

A number of topics lend themselves well to information grids, but some possible topics include basic introductions (e.g., when you have a new group of students and you want them to get to know each other), work details (where they work, what their jobs are, how long they have been there), transportation (whether they drive, when they take the bus/train, etc.), health (what they do when they have a stomachache, when they go to the doctor), and travel (what countries they have visited, where they want to visit).

Activity 50 — *Information Grids—Basic Steps*
(beginning, intermediate)

PURPOSE

To enable students to communicate basic information about themselves and to request similar information from others, both orally and in writing.

METHOD

The steps below constitute the basic two-part teaching technique to use for most information grids.

Create the grid

1. Select a topic for the grid.

   Example: Introductions

2. Select the column headings you want to use.

3. Create the grid on a blackboard or whiteboard, overhead transparency, computer screen with a projector, or sheet of flip chart paper so that all the students can see it. In the left-hand column, write a number for each student in the group. The example on the following page is set up for a group of six students. You can make copies of the blank grid on page 146 for students to use or have them draw similar grids in their notebooks.

4. Select a student. Write his or her name on the first line as you repeat the name slowly and clearly.

5. Ask the student questions, and write simplified versions of the answers.

   Examples:

   "Where are you from?"
   (Instead of writing "He is from Chile," you can just write "Chile.")
   "How long have you been in the United States?"

6. Write the student's responses on the grid. Read aloud what you have written.

7. Repeat this process with two other students.

8. When you have completed the chart for the first three students, select two others to work as partners. Ask one partner to interview the other using the same questions that you have been asking. ("Margaret, ask the same questions of Carlos, please.") Write the person's name and responses on the grid.

9. Ask the partners to reverse roles and repeat the interview process. Write the new name and responses on the grid.

10. Ask for a volunteer to interview a student who hasn't yet been involved. Write the student's name and responses on the grid. Encourage students to ask you questions as well, and write your answers.

    (If you have a large group, do not create a grid that will include everyone. Limit it to five or six students. You will be able to involve the rest of the students in steps 12–14.)

Name	Homeland	Length of Time in United States	Married or Single	Number of Children
1. Miecko	Japan	6 months	M	1
2. Pedro	Mexico	2 months	S	0
3. Dagoberto	Chile	1 year	M	3
4. Monisha	India	9 months	M	1
5. Diego	Mexico	2 years	S	0
6. Trang	Vietnam	1 year	S	0

11. Review the information on the grid, including each person's name. This is especially important for beginning-level students and those who might have difficulty reading some of the words.

TEACHING ADULTS: AN ESL RESOURCE BOOK

Ask questions about the grid

Once the grid has been completed, you can ask any number of questions that require the students to read and understand the information shown on the grid.

12. Ask some simple questions that can be answered directly from the information shown on the grid. Examples:

> "Who is from [Country]?"
>
> "How long has [Name] been in the United States?"
>
> "Is [Name] married?"
>
> "How many children does [Name] have?"
>
> "Who has three children?"

Each time you ask a question, allow plenty of time before you call on someone to answer it. This ensures that all students will think about how to answer the question.

13. Select a student to ask another student a question based on the grid. Repeat this procedure, giving each student a chance to ask and answer at least one question.

14. Ask summary questions about the grid. Examples:

> "How many people in the class are single?"
>
> "How many people in the class have children?"
>
> "How many are from Mexico?"
>
> "Who has been in the United States for more than a year?"

SUGGESTIONS

- When creating a grid for beginners, ask each student the same question before moving on to the next question. For example, in the above grid, write the first student's name, and ask her where she is from. Then write the other students' names in turn, asking each to answer the same question. Return to the first student to ask how long she has been in the United States. Ask each of the other students this question, and so on. When you are ready to have the students try asking the questions, have each person ask only one question. For example, you can say, "Wong, ask Farah where he is from" rather than "Wong, ask Farah all these questions."

- To create a more interactive activity, select a topic and write the column headings and numbers on a piece of paper. Make a copy for each student in the group. Have the students complete their own grids by circulating and interviewing each other. Before they begin, review the kinds of questions they will need to ask to complete their grids, give students a chance to practice articulating each question, and coach pronunciation, if necessary.

- In a multilevel ESL class, have the higher-level students ask the lower-level students questions based on the information in the grid.

- If students have begun to work on writing, ask each student to use information from the completed grid to write sentences about other people in the group. ("Write a sentence about Marta and how long she has been in the United States.") If students have difficulty writing sentences by themselves, you can do the writing as they dictate the sentences. The students can then copy these.

- Use information grids to poll the likes and dislikes to help them see how they are similar and different. For example, list the students' names down the left-hand side of the grid. List the names of various sports across the top as column headings (*Football, Baseball, Basketball, Soccer, Swimming*). Put a plus (+) or a minus (–) under each heading to show whether an individual student likes or dislikes that sport.

- Use an information grid as a pre-reading activity to help the students see what they already know about the topic of the reading text or to introduce key vocabulary that will be used in it. For example, if the students will be reading about different occupations, you might want to prepare them by creating a grid that can help them talk about their own jobs. Example:

Jobs					
Name	Occupation	Deal with Public?	Indoors or Outdoors?	Need Training?	How Long in Job?
1.					
2.					
3.					

51   *Information Grids to Meet Real-Life Needs* (all)

PURPOSE

To prepare students to provide information about themselves that will be required in specific real-life situations.

METHOD

Use the steps described in Activity 50 to help students create and discuss grids that prepare them to handle specific real-life situations. An example of this type of grid follows:

Example: Preparing to fill out a job application

Job Application					
Name	Job Wanted	Years of Experience	Previous Job	Name of Previous Manager	Previous Manager's Phone Number
1.					
2.					
3.					
4.					
5.					
6.					

© New Readers Press. All rights reserved.

CHAPTER 7: INTEGRATED COMMUNICATION ACTIVITIES   **149**

Activity 52

Information Grids to Review and Reinforce Specific Grammatical Structures or Vocabulary
(intermediate)

PURPOSE

To reinforce specific grammatical structures or vocabulary and to generate conversation about how students are alike or different.

METHOD

1. Use the steps described in Activity 50 to help students create a grid that reinforces the grammar and vocabulary they are studying and to generate conversation. You can use almost any topic. The sample below is for a group that has been discussing time, the use of the abbreviations *a.m.* and *p.m.*, and the use of the simple present tense ("I get up" vs. "I am getting up").

What Time Do You . . . ?				
Name	**Go to Bed**	**Get Up**	**Eat Breakfast**	**Leave for Work**
1. Maria	10:00 p.m.	6:30 a.m.	yes	7:15 a.m.
2. Wong	11:00 p.m.	6:00 a.m.	yes	7:00 a.m.
3. Luis	11:30 p.m.	7:00 a.m.	no	8:00 a.m.
4. Ivan	9:00 a.m.	4:00 p.m.	yes	10:30 p.m.
5. Frieda	9:30 p.m.	6:00 a.m.	no	6:30 a.m.

2. Ask questions that students can answer directly from the grid. Examples:

> "What time does Frieda go to bed?"
>
> "How many people get up at 6:00 a.m.?"
>
> "Who leaves for work at night?"
>
> "Who leaves for work last in the morning?"

3. Ask more difficult questions that require students to manipulate the information in the grid. Examples:

"Who goes to bed the earliest?"

"How many students eat breakfast every morning?"

"How many students go to work before 9:00 a.m.?"

Information Grids in One-to-One Tutoring
(beginning, intermediate)

Activity 53

PURPOSE

To practice conversational English on various life-skill topics with the use of an information grid.

METHOD

There are several ways to adapt information grids for use in one-to-one learning situations:

- Use the same grid as the one shown on page 145. Put the headings on the top line. On the left-hand side, list names of three people the student knows well, such as family members or friends. Then list names of three people you know (preferably people who were not born in the United States). Ask the student the questions necessary to enable you to complete his or her part of the grid. Then complete your own part as you talk about the people you know. ("My friend Dagny is from Denmark. She has been in this country for 75 years.") When you complete the grid, ask questions such as the following:

"How long has my friend Dagny been in this country?"

"How many children does my sister have?"

"How many people are from Asia?"

"Who has been in this country longer—your sister Maria or my friend Stefan?"

- Depending on where you meet for tutoring, have the student ask information grid questions of staff members or others nearby. If you meet in a library, for example, the student can ask library staff members. Both this idea and the one that follows will require some instruction in how to request information (e.g., "Excuse me. May I ask you some questions for an English activity?"). This also boosts confidence by giving students practice with native speakers of English.

- Assign the information grid for homework. Have the student ask the questions of others at work, at home, or in other settings.

- Create a grid that lists something in the left-hand column other than people's names. An example might be a grid about transportation. The purpose of completing the grid might be to have students understand and practice using the words *often, sometimes, not often,* and *never*.

How often do you use these?				
Type	Often	Sometimes	Not Often	Never
1. Bicycle				
2. Car				
3. Bus				
4. Subway				
5. Train				
6. Plane				

Information Gap

Information gap activities require students to use their English language skills to share information to complete a task—a true communicative task. The students cannot complete the task with the information they have at the beginning of the activity.

During the activity, students interact to exchange information for a real purpose—this is exactly the way people use language in real life. Students are not merely parroting phrases and sentences that the tutor or teacher says, nor are they asking questions to which they already know the answers. ("Maria, ask Wong what his name is and if he is studying English.") Instead, students are asking their own questions, giving commands, and giving and receiving *information that is new to them.*

An information gap activity is always used as a follow-up or practice activity and should not be used to introduce new material. Before beginning the activity, be sure that you have already introduced the vocabulary and grammatical structures that students will encounter.

The following activities require students to use listening, speaking, reading, and writing to fill information gaps.

Activity 54

Supermarket Ad (beginning, intermediate)

PURPOSE

To practice reading a grocery store shopping ad in an information gap activity.

METHOD

1. Collect supermarket ads that advertise a variety of different food products. You will need two copies of each ad. (If you don't have a second copy, make a photocopy.)

2. Make two copies of a shopping list with two columns. At the top of the first column, write the heading *Item.* At the top of the second column, write the heading *Price.* In the first column, write the names of eight foods that are listed in the ad. Leave the price column blank. See the example below.

Item	Price
orange juice	
bread	
apples	
chicken	
hot dogs	
tomatoes	
rice	
carrots	

3. On one copy of the ad, use a marker to black out the price of four items that are on the shopping list. On the second copy of the ad, black out the prices of the other four items that are on the shopping list.

4. Prepare one set of materials (two copies of an ad with different sets of prices blacked out and two copies of the related shopping list) for each pair of students. Use a different ad for each pair. The ads should all contain some of the same food items, however.

5. Give the set of materials to each pair of students. Ask each person to take one copy of the ad but not to show it to his or her partner.

TEACHING ADULTS: AN ESL RESOURCE BOOK

6. Ask each student to find in the ad the foods that appear in the shopping list. They should then fill in the shopping list with as many prices as possible. Explain that they need to include any special information related to the price. Examples: Whether the orange juice price is for a 6- or 12-ounce can, whether the carrot price is for one pound or three pounds.

7. Explain that the students will not be able to fill in all the prices by themselves. Tell them that they must ask their partner questions in order to fill in the remaining prices. (They cannot simply look at each other's ad; you could give students file folders to put their ads in so the ads are not visible to the partner.) The partner should give the price and any additional information necessary. Example:

> "How much is the chicken?"
>
> "The chicken is three dollars and fifty cents a pound."

8. When the students have filled in all the prices on their shopping lists, select one person to read his or her shopping list aloud to the group (items and prices). Ask the other pairs to listen to see if they have any of the same items on their shopping lists.

9. Ask pairs who had the same items to tell the group whether their prices were the same or different.

SUGGESTION

- Use the activity to review food categories. For example, ask each student to write the word *fruits* on a sheet of paper and then list all the fruits named in the ad.

Activity 55

Venn Diagram (all)

PURPOSE

To use a Venn diagram to find out what students can do.

METHOD

1. Divide the group into pairs. If you are in a one-to-one situation, you and the student can work together. Tell students they will work with a partner to complete the statement "I can...".

2. Create a Venn diagram like the following on an 8½" × 11" piece of paper. Make one copy for each pair.

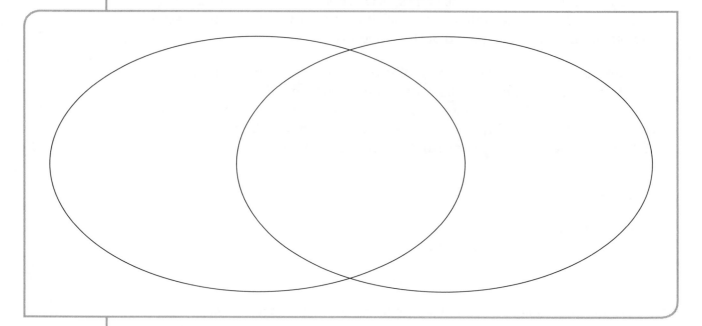

3. Tell the partners they must work together to complete the diagram. Give them these instructions:

"On the left side, write three things that you can do (such as cook chicken, play soccer, or paint) but your partner cannot do. Ask questions to find your partner's answers."

"On the right side, write three things that your partner can do but you cannot do. Again, ask questions to find your partner's answers."

"In the middle, write three things that both of you can do."

Walk around to make sure students are filling out their diagrams correctly.

4. When students are finished, write the following on the board:

I was surprised to learn that . . .

5. Call on a few of the students to complete this sentence.

6. Ask for volunteers to tell the rest of the class what they learned about their partners.

SUGGESTIONS

- If the partners are still continuing their discussion in English after the allotted time, you can let the activity run longer—even if they have completed the chart. This activity is an effective conversation starter that often results in lively, animated discussion about the things that students can and cannot do.

- One variation of this activity would be to use a Johari Window (see below). You would expand the instructions to include a fourth area.

Both A and B	Only A
Only B	Neither A nor B

- You can vary the activity by using different sentence beginnings:

I have/don't have . . .
I like/don't like . . .
I am/am not . . .
I have/have never . . .
Every day I . . .

(Johari window idea adapted from Richard and Marjorie Baudains, *Alternatives: Games, Exercises and Conversations for the Language Classroom,* © 1990 by Longman Group Ltd. Used with permission.)

Other Integrated Communication Activities

Activity 56 — "I'm a Banana. What Are You?"
(beginning, intermediate)

PURPOSES

To review recently taught vocabulary.

To get students to stand up and "re-energize."

To divide a large group into smaller groups.

METHOD

1. Decide how many categories of objects you want and what the categories will be. Examples: *fruits, cooking utensils, vegetables, clothing*. (If you are using the activity as a fun way to divide the students into a specific number of small groups, use that number of categories.)

2. Make a list of items for each category. The total number of items needs to equal the number of students in the group. (Each category should have approximately the same number of items.) Example (for a group of 16 students):

Fruits:	banana, apple, pear, orange
Cooking utensils:	frying pan, spatula, eggbeater, measuring cup
Vegetables:	carrot, cabbage, onion, potato
Clothing:	shoe, jacket, shirt, hat

3. Give each student an index card on which you have written the name of one of these items. (Do not write the category names on these cards.)

4. Ask students to get up and walk around the room. As they approach other students, they should say, "I'm a [item listed on their card]. What are you?" The objective is to find all the other students who belong in the same category as they do.

5. When the students have found the others in their category, ask them to sit together and write a list of all the items they can think of in that category. Give them three or four minutes for this part of the activity.

6. When the time is up, ask a member of each group to tell what category the group members belong to and to read aloud the items they wrote on their list.

SUGGESTION

- Give students extra time to continue their conversations if they seem interested in what they are discussing. As long as students are speaking English, this sort of "free" conversation should be encouraged.

Teaching Basic Computer Use
(beginning, low-intermediate)

PURPOSES

To help students start to use computers.

To help students write short stories about themselves on a computer.

METHOD

1. Ask your student if he or she has used a computer. If there is some previous experience, ask, "When did you use a computer? Why? What did you do on the computer? Did you use the Internet? What did you do on the Internet?"

2. Give your student a copy of the handout on the next page.

   Work with your student to label each of the parts of a computer (as in the handout). The words to fill in will be as follows (definitions you can provide appear here in parentheses):

---

1. monitor/screen (where you can see the information on the computer—similar to a TV screen)
2. CPU (short for central processing unit—the computer "brain" or where the computer stores information)
3. keyboard (used for typing)
4. mouse (for computer navigation)
5. laptop (a portable computer)
6. USB drive (can store files and connect to the computer)
7. headphones (used for listening)

On lines 8–10, review the new words and their definitions. Have the student repeat each new word several times to become familiar with pronunciation.

Basic Computer Use

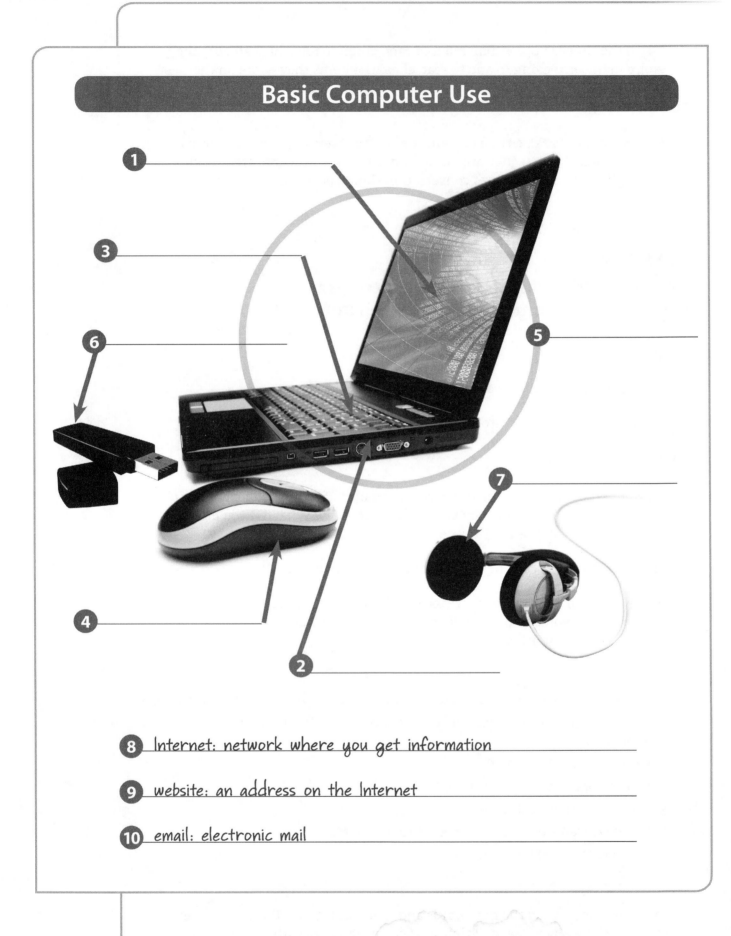

8. Internet: network where you get information

9. website: an address on the Internet

10. email: electronic mail

TEACHING ADULTS: AN ESL RESOURCE BOOK

3. Have your student sit in front of a real computer. If you are in a small group versus one-to-one, you can pair experienced computer users with less experienced ones. On the computer, point to the various parts that you have taught, and ask your student to name these parts for you.

4. If a student has very little computer experience, guide him or her to the website Mousercise to practice how to use a mouse. The website's URL is **http://www.pbclibrary.org/mousing/mousercise.htm**. You will probably need to help a beginning student type in the URL. Have the student click on "Let's start mousercising" and then click on the various numbers that the exercise includes.

5. Once students feel more comfortable with a mouse, have them practice with you using a word processing program such as Microsoft Word to write about themselves. Show the screen for your computer's word processing program. Point out a few important keys on the keyboard, such as the delete/backspace key, the space bar, the arrow keys, the shift key for making capital letters, and the enter/return key. You can briefly address what each key does. As you work through the following exercise, keep in mind that the goal is to get the student comfortable using the keyboard, not to master the use of those keys.

   To give keyboard practice, ask the student to type his or her first and last names. Tell about the space bar to separate first and last names. Then the student can use the back arrow, delete, and shift keys to capitalize the first name. He or she can use the forward arrow, delete, and shift to capitalize the last name. Have the student hold down one letter and watch how it repeats across the screen and wraps to the next line. This will happen when writing as well. When the student wants to go to a new line or start a new paragraph, he or she can hit return. Practice this.

6. Give your student a model of the story you want him or her to write. For example, if your student is at a high-beginning level, the model might look like this:

> My name is *John Lopez*. I am from *Mexico*. I live in *Tampa*. I am a *painter*. I have *two children*.

   Alternately, you can write a story about yourself to share. Encourage your student to write more if possible.

7. Provide help as needed as your student writes the story. Remind him or her to use the word processing keys such as space bar and backspace/delete. Provide assistance to correct major errors.

8. If you have access to a printer, help your student print the story. You can use the story for further reading and expansion practice, such as cloze activities.

(Activity adapted from "Basic Computer Use," *Notebook*, Spring 2011, pp. 9–10.)

SUGGESTIONS

- Connect students to the "real world" by helping them get library cards. If you are familiar with the library, show them around or ask a staff member to do so. See if the library has classes in a topic that might interest a student, such as using computers.

- Go on a field trip. In addition to the library, going to supermarkets, malls, museums, performances, and culture sights will give students authentic language practice.

- Ask students what they think of your lessons. This gives them a chance to reflect on what they are learning and gives you a chance to improve your lessons (or confirm that what you are doing is on target). Some questions you might want to ask:

  ▷ Are the lessons very easy or very hard?

  ▷ Am I speaking too fast for you (or using too many difficult words)?

  ▷ What have you learned in the last few weeks during our lessons?

  ▷ What has been the most useful thing you have learned?

  ▷ What would you like to learn more about?

- If the student likes to cook, see if he or she will give you a cooking lesson.

- Collect forms wherever you go, and have your student practice filling them out. These forms might include job applications, bank forms, doctor's office forms, credit card applications, etc. If a student will use one of those forms in a real-world context soon, encourage him or her to hold on to that form and take it home. This will make it much easier for him or her to fill out the "real" form.

- Get permission from your student to talk to his or her manager at work to get suggestions for specific topics or language skills to work on.

- If the student has children in school, see if you can arrange for you and your student to visit and observe what goes on during the day. Have a debriefing session afterward to answer questions your student might have about the school system.

(Courtesy of Lynne Weintraub.)

Pulling It All Together: Lesson Planning

A lesson plan helps you decide in advance what skills to work on and what materials and activities to use during the lesson. It provides you with a structure for the lesson—showing not only what you and the student will do but also how long the lesson is and in what order it is taught. In addition, the lesson plan becomes a record of what you have taught and may come in handy as a reference when you are designing future lessons.

Two Ingredients of a Lesson Plan

In creating a lesson plan, you will usually need to allow time in the lesson for both of the following:

1. Work in the core instructional materials or series

    A published ESL instructional series such as *Lifeskills, English No Problem!* or *Laubach Way to English* helps you to teach the basic English skills that all ESL students must develop, whatever their individual needs or interests. Examples of this include the ability to greet someone, to ask for directions, or to find a phone number online or in a telephone book. Using a well-designed instructional series will also help you feel more confident: You won't have to worry about missing any key skills. It will also save you time since you won't have to create all the activities from scratch.

2. Activities designed to meet students' individual needs

    In this part of the lesson, you will be addressing the *individual* needs that you identified when you did the learners' needs assessments (see Chapter 4). Examples:

    *   For students who are in a workplace setting: learning to read the words on a parts inventory

- For students who are parents of young children: learning how to communicate with their children's teachers

- For students who depend on public transportation: learning how to find information about bus schedules

- For students who wish to become U.S. citizens: learning specific civics, literacy, and interview questions for the test

Steps in Lesson Planning

To plan the part of the lesson that will address students' individual needs, simply ask the three questions *Who? What?* and *How?*

The following example is for a tutor who is working in a one-to-one situation. If you are working with a group of students, try to identify needs that are common to all or many of the students. Sometimes you will choose to address a need that was identified by only one or two students. When doing so, try to ensure that the discussion and practice will also be useful to the others. If one student has a very specific or immediate need, set aside some time to work with that person after class.

Ask Who?

The following profile was developed from information obtained during the initial needs assessment and from a very preliminary evaluation of the learner's English skills. It shows how one tutor answered *Who?* for the learner Song Chann.

You can use the information in the profile to develop learning objectives. Learning objectives tell what the student will learn or be able to do by the end of the lesson (or several lessons). The objectives should be specific and focused rather than general. They should be written in such a way that it will be easy to tell when the learner has met the objectives. Examples of specific objectives for Song Chann might include the following:

1. She will know vocabulary related to office cleaning.

2. She will be able to talk about her daily routine so she can discuss scheduling for work and family responsibilities.

3. She will be able to tell someone about the members of her family.

Student Profile: Song Chann	
Approximate age:	early 20s
Homeland:	Cambodia
Length of time in United States:	one year
Family:	husband (housepainter) two daughters (2 and 4 years old)
Job in United States:	office cleaning (part-time, evenings)
Work experience in homeland:	seamstress
Education:	high school graduate (Cambodia)
Personal interests:	sewing, singing, painting
Goal:	to become a nurse
Reasons for learning English:	to communicate with English-speaking coworkers at her current cleaning job to enter nursing school
English skills:	studied English in Cambodia but speaks only a little understands some English if spoken slowly

Student Profile: _____	
Approximate age:	
Homeland:	
Length of time in United States:	
Family:	
Job in United States:	
Work experience in homeland:	
Education:	
Personal interests:	
Goal:	
Reasons for learning English:	
English skills:	

When developing learning objectives, think about what happened in previous lessons, if applicable. For example, did the student share her frustration at not being able to understand someone on the telephone? Did she start to tell you about a special dish she likes to prepare but then stopped because she didn't know the English names of the ingredients? Think of such unplanned-for events as "teachable moments," and take advantage of them whenever they happen—even if you have to set aside something else that you had planned to do during the lesson. These are golden opportunities to teach something that the learner considers important. If appropriate, you can develop objectives for future lessons that build on this learning.

After you present what you want to teach for a given objective, you can see if the student has actually met the objective. If not, you may want to simplify the material or try teaching the objective again at a later time.

Step 2

Ask What?

For each objective, ask *What?*: "What topics and language skills do we need to address to meet this objective?"

For example, Song Chann's tutor might choose the topic of "Daily Routines" to address the second objective. She will then identify relevant vocabulary. Sometimes this vocabulary may be based on a textbook reading. The sample lesson plan in this chapter, for instance, uses a story from *What's Next?* that includes some common routine-related words: *get up, fix breakfast, drink, dishes.* At other times, the vocabulary may be drawn from a picture dictionary entry on a relevant topic. Sometimes a tutor will have to work alone or with the student to identify relevant vocabulary for study. Most lessons will also involve language skills, such as asking questions or giving information.

Step 3

Ask How?

Ask yourself, "How will I teach these skills?" This will help you select the appropriate materials and activities for teaching the new vocabulary and language skills.

After you answer these three questions, you will be able to create a lesson plan outline like the one that follows.

TEACHING ADULTS: AN ESL RESOURCE BOOK

Lesson Plan Outline: Song Chann	
Learning objective:	Song Chann will be able to communicate about her daily routine.
Topic:	morning routine
Language skills:	vocabulary: *Monday, gets up, fixes, breakfast, dishes*
Activities:	vocabulary: • use props and the story to introduce vocabulary • practice vocabulary with textbook-based exercises writing: write an LEA story about Song's morning routine
Materials:	objects (or pictures): kitchen utensils, a pot or pan, breakfast food, a calendar, a toothbrush; a copy of the Daily Routines pages from *The Oxford Picture Dictionary*

Step 4

Write the Lesson Plan

The next step is to plan out the specific steps you will follow for each activity in the session. You can use the "Lesson Plan Activity Sheet" form on page 171 to do this. See pages 169–170 for a sample of a lesson plan that the tutor used with Song Chann after they had met several times.

As you look at the completed lesson plan, note the following.

FREE CONVERSATION

Try to start each lesson with a few minutes of free conversation. This gives the student an opportunity to ease into English during the first few minutes of the session without having to worry about learning anything new. It allows the student to use English to communicate and to gain valuable practice in choosing what he or she wants to say in an informal social situation. It also gives you insights into the student's daily life and can give you new ideas about other language needs—both obvious and not so obvious—that the student may have. Do not correct the student's errors during free conversation.

Try to end your lessons with free conversation as well. To get started, you might ask what your student plans to do during the coming week.

REVIEW

Always build in time to review what you taught in previous lessons. You will notice that the sample lesson plan reviews and builds upon information from the previous lesson. Recycling information is essential in language acquisition. You might choose to review a specific segment of a previous lesson or reuse vocabulary or grammatical structures in new activities.

NOTES

Take careful notes. You can use the "Notes" section on the "Lesson Plan Activity Sheets" to record

- what you actually covered. (You might not always be able to carry out everything you included in the lesson plan. That's fine. You should always take the time to respond to unexpected questions or needs that arise during the lesson.)

- unplanned topics that came up during a lesson.

- ideas for topics or activities that you want to include in the next lesson(s). (It's always better to have too much material and not be able to use it all than to have too little material to cover.)

VARIETY

Use a variety of activities in the lesson. For instance, the sample lesson plan for Song Chann begins with a TPR activity to teach the names of pieces of cleaning equipment. Then the tutor introduces a dialogue incorporating questions about the location of this equipment. In a follow-up role play, Song Chann has an opportunity to ask similar questions or to give the information to others using additional English that she knows. The tutor then uses props, textbook practice, and a story Song writes based on her morning routine as ways to practice new vocabulary and life skills related to reporting daily routines.

REASSESSMENT

Periodically include time for reassessment of the student's interests, goals, and language skills. You can also use this time to practice material taught a few lessons back. This helps to constantly reinforce what you want the student to learn and retain.

Sample of Completed Lesson Plan Activity Sheet

LEARNER Song Chann   **DATE** November 8

LENGTH OF LESSON 90 minutes

Activity	Materials	Time	Notes
1. Free conversation		5 min.	
2. Questions to review previous lesson "What is May doing?" "Where do you clean?" "What do you use to clean?"	previous lesson plan	5 min.	
3. Cleaning the office Total Physical Response	mop duster broom picture of office *The Oxford Picture Dictionary*	5 min.	
4. Teach questions "Where is the _____?" "May I have the _____?"	same as #3 above	10 min.	
5. Dialogue and role play supply room	dialogue: A: Excuse me? B: Yes? A: Where is the supply room? B: Just down the hall. A: Can I get a broom there? B: Yeah, I think so. A: Thank you.	10 min.	

Sample of Completed Lesson Plan Activity Sheet (continued)

LEARNER Song Chann   **DATE** November 8

LENGTH OF LESSON 90 minutes

Activity	Materials	Time	Notes
6. *What's Next?* series "Warm-up" ask about morning routine to see what vocabulary Song knows and what still needs to be taught "Presentation"	*What's Next?* Low Beginning, Book 1, p. 28 Teacher's Edition, pp. 19–21 props or pictures: kitchen utensils, newspaper, breakfast pictures, any other items someone might use in the morning	15 min.	
7. Create an LEA story about Song's morning routine	based on story on p. 28 of *What's Next?* Low Beginning, Book 1	15 min.	
8. Reading and writing Check story comprehension and practice new vocabulary with sentence writing	*What's Next?* Low Beginning, Book 1, pp. 29–31	20 min.	
9. Free conversation		5 min.	

Lesson Plan Activity Sheet

LEARNER _____   **DATE** _____

LENGTH OF LESSON _____

Activity	Materials	Time	Notes

Appendix

The Sounds of English

If you understand how speech sounds are made, you will be able to describe what a student needs to do in order to pronounce the sounds correctly.

Consonant Sounds

The Consonant Sounds chart indicates which parts of the speech mechanism are used to produce English consonant sounds and how the sounds are produced.

Note that the letter in slashes / / in the first column represents the sound—not the letter. This sound can often be spelled in different ways. It can also appear in different positions within a word. Examples of both of these are included in the second column.

The following codes are used in the third column to describe the sounds:

> v = voiced (vocal cords vibrate)
>
> un = unvoiced (vocal cords do not vibrate)
>
> c = continuant (sound can be continued as long as the speaker has breath)
>
> s = stop (sound cannot be continued)
>
> n = nasal (sound comes through the nose)

Consonant Sounds

Sound	As In	Code	How Sound Is Made
/b/	**b**ird, kno**b**	v, s	Stop air with lips together; open with small puff of breath. Voiced equivalent of /p/.
/p/	**p**an, sna**p**	un, s	Stop air with lips together; open with a big puff of breath. Unvoiced equivalent of /b/.
/d/	**d**ish, roa**d**	v, s	Lips and teeth slightly parted. Stop air with tongue tip touching the roof of the mouth just behind the upper teeth. Tongue is dropped as breath is expelled. Voiced equivalent of /t/.
/t/	**t**ent, mel**t**, mi**tt**	un, s	Lips and teeth slightly parted. Stop air with tongue tip touching the roof of the mouth just behind the upper teeth. Tongue is dropped as breath is expelled. Unvoiced equivalent of /d/.
/v/	**v**alley, ha**v**e	v, c	Lower lip touching upper teeth lightly. Air passes between the lip and teeth. Voiced equivalent of /f/.
/f/	**f**ish, **ph**one, tou**gh**, sta**ff**	un, c	Lower lip touching upper teeth lightly. Air passes between the lip and teeth. Unvoiced equivalent of /v/.
/th/	**th**e, brea**th**e	v, c	Tongue touches both upper and lower teeth and may be slightly inserted between teeth. Air passes through the opening formed by tongue and upper teeth. Voiced equivalent of /th/.
/th/	**th**anks, four**th**	un, c	Tongue touches both upper and lower teeth and may be slightly inserted between teeth. Air passes through the opening formed by tongue and upper teeth. Unvoiced equivalent of /th/.
/z/	**z**ipper, qui**z**, hi**s**, teache**s**, kid**s**, fu**zz**	v, c	Teeth close but not touching. Tongue tip approaches roof of mouth just behind the upper teeth, making a narrow opening. Air streams through this opening. Voiced equivalent of /s/.
/s/	**s**nake, **c**ity, mi**c**e, bi**c**ycle, ba**ss**	un, c	Teeth close but not touching. Tongue tip approaches roof of mouth just behind the upper teeth, making a narrow opening. Air streams through this opening. Unvoiced equivalent of /z/.

Sound	As In	Code	How Sound Is Made
/zh/	mea**s**ure, televi**si**on, fi**ss**ion, a**z**ure, re**g**ime	v, c	Lips forward and squared. Teeth close but not touching. Tongue tip close to middle of roof of mouth. Tongue sides are up, forming a groove. Air passes through the groove. Voiced equivalent of /sh/.
/sh/	**sh**op, bu**sh**, **Ch**icago, mi**ss**ion, cap**ti**on, **s**ure	un, c	Lips forward and squared. Teeth close but not touching. Tongue tip close to middle of roof of mouth. Tongue sides are up, forming a groove. Air passes through the groove. Unvoiced equivalent of /zh/.
/j/	**j**ump, **g**entle, fu**dge**	v, s + c	A combination of /d/ and /zh/. Lips forward. Start with tongue tip touching the roof of the mouth behind the teeth (in the position for making /d/). Stop the air; then release as a continuant. Voiced equivalent of /ch/.
/ch/	**ch**ildren, kit**ch**en, mu**ch**	un, s + c	A combination of /t/ and /sh/. Lips forward. Start with tongue tip touching the roof of the mouth behind the teeth (in the position for making /t/). Stop the air; then release as a continuant. Unvoiced equivalent of /j/.
/g/	**g**irl, le**g**	v, s	Tongue tip down. Back of tongue touching the roof of the mouth to stop the flow of air. Back of tongue is dropped as breath is released. Voiced equivalent of /k/.
/k/	**k**itchen, mar**k**, si**ck**, **c**up, **Ch**ris	un, s	Tongue tip down. Back of tongue touching the roof of the mouth to stop the flow of air. Back of tongue is dropped as breath is released. Unvoiced equivalent of /g/.
/l/	**l**eg, ro**ll**, babb**le**	v, c	Tongue tip touches the roof of the mouth just behind the upper teeth. Air comes out along the side(s) of the tongue. This is a voiced sound.
/r/	**r**ive**r**, **wr**ap	v, c	Tongue tip up—near the front of the roof of the mouth, but not touching. Lips forward and squared. Air passes over the top of the tongue. This is a voiced sound.
/h/	**h**and, be**h**ind	un, c	Has no position of its own. Position the tongue for the vowel following it and give breath sound with no voicing.

Sound	As In	Code	How Sound Is Made
/w/	**w**oman, re**w**ard	v, c	Lips forward and rounded. Air passes through opening. Tongue is in a neutral position. This is a voiced sound.
/y/	**y**ells, **u**se (/**y**ooz/)	v, c	Lips relaxed; teeth close together. Middle of tongue moves toward roof of mouth without touching. Air passes over the top of the tongue. This is a voiced sound.
/m/	**m**an, le**m**on, sa**me**	v, c, n	Lips together. Air passes through the nasal cavity instead of the mouth. This is a voiced sound.
/n/	**n**eck, ca**n**al, fi**ne**, **gn**aw, **kn**ock, A**nn**	v, c, n	Lips and teeth slightly parted. Tongue tip touching the roof of the mouth just behind upper teeth. Air passes through nasal cavity instead of mouth. This is a voiced sound.
/ng/	ri**ng**	v, c, n	Lips open. Back of tongue touches back of roof of mouth. Air passes through the nasal cavity instead of the mouth. This is a voiced sound.
/hw/	**wh**istle	un, c	Lips rounded in preparation for /w/ sound. Sound starts with breath as in production of /h/ sound and finishes as /w/. *Note:* Many English speakers do not use this sound.

Combination Sounds with /k/

/k/ + /w/	**qu**arter, ac**qu**aint	(un, s) + (v, c)	See /k/ and /w/. The two sounds are produced one after the other in combination. In written English, *q* is always followed by *u* except for some foreign words such as *Qatar* and *Aqaba*. However, in these cases, the sound is /k/, not /k/ + /w/.
/k/ + /s/	bo**x**, loo**ks**, pic**ks**	(un, s) + (un, c)	See /k/ and /s/. The two sounds are produced one after the other in combination.

Vowel Sounds

All vowel sounds are voiced continuants. They can be described by

- where in the mouth the tongue forms a hump.

- whether the lips are rounded or unrounded.

- whether the muscles of the lips and tongue are tense (tightened slightly) or lax (relaxed).

The best way to describe how a vowel sound is made is to indicate the position of the tongue hump. The following chart shows where the tongue hump is positioned for each of the English vowel sounds.*

	Front	Central	Back
High	/ē/ beat /i/ bit		/oo/ boot /uu/ book
Mid	/ā/ bait /e/ bet	/er/ bird /u/ but	/ō/ boat /aw/ bought
Low	/a/ bat	/o/ pot	

* Some vowel classification systems include a symbol for the vowel sound in words like *few* or **use**. In this book, the sound is not described separately. It is considered a combination of the consonant sound /y/ and the vowel sound /oo/.

Try the following suggestions if you (or the students) have difficulty distinguishing between high/low, front/back, unrounded/rounded, or tense/lax vowels:

- Say the front vowels in order from high to low: /ē/, /i/, /ā/, /e/, /a/. Notice that your mouth opens wider as you move through the list. Also notice that the hump made by your tongue stays in a front position. Say the back vowels /oo/, /uu/, /ō/, /aw/. Notice that the hump stays in a back position.

- Say the two high sounds /ē/ and /oo/ several times. Notice that the tongue hump moves from the front of the mouth to the back of the mouth. Notice also that the lips are unrounded when you say /ē/ and rounded when you say /oo/. Try this with the two mid sounds /ā/ and /ō/.

- Say the two front sounds /ē/ and /i/ several times. Notice that the muscles of the lips move from being tense to being lax. Try this with the following pairs: /ā/ and /e/, and /oo/ and /uu/.

The Vowel Sounds chart describes how each English vowel sound is produced—where the tongue hump is located and whether there is tenseness/laxness or unrounding/rounding during production of the sound.

Vowel Sounds

Sound	As In	Code	How Sound Is Made
Front			
/ē/	b**ea**t, **ee**l, w**e**, St**e**ve, k**ey**	v, c	high/front, tense, unrounded
/i/	b**i**t, L**y**nn, **if**	v, c	lower high/front, lax, unrounded
/ā/	b**ai**t, r**a**te, s**ay**	v, c	mid/front, tense, unrounded
/e/	b**e**t, f**ea**ther	v, c	lower mid/front, lax, unrounded
/a/	b**a**t, **a**fter	v, c	low/front, lax, unrounded
Central			
/er/	b**ir**d, h**er**, b**ur**n	v, c	mid/central, tense, lips forward and almost squared
/u/	b**u**t, fr**o**m, t**ou**gh	v, c	lower mid/central, lax, unrounded (In an unstressed syllable such as *a-bove*, this sound is referred to as the "schwa" /ə/.)
/o/	**o**live, p**o**t, f**a**ther	v, c	low/central, lax, unrounded
Back			
/oo/	b**oo**t, fl**u**te, bl**ue**, ch**ew**	v, c	high/back, tense, rounded
/uu/	b**oo**k, b**u**sh, c**ou**ld	v, c	lower high/back, lax, rounded
/ō/	b**oa**t, h**o**pe, sl**ow**, g**o**	v, c	mid/back, tense, rounded
/aw/	s**aw**, b**ou**ght, P**au**l, t**augh**t	v, c	lower mid/back, lax, rounded

A diphthong is a vowel sound that starts out as one vowel and moves to another vowel sound position.

Diphthongs

Sound	As In	Code	How Sound Is Made
/ai/	**i**vory, **I**, f**i**ve, n**igh**t, t**ie**	v, c	Starts out as /o/ (low/central) as in *pot* and moves to /i/ (lower high/front) as in *bit*
/oi/	b**oy**, b**oi**l	v, c	Starts out as /ō/ (mid/back) as in *boat* and moves to /i/ (lower high/front) as in *bit*
/ou/	h**ou**se, h**ow**	v, c	Starts out as /o/ (low/central) as in *pot* and moves to /uu/ (lower high/back) as in *book*

B

Appendix

Considering Assessment

Many programs regularly assess students before and after they complete a class. These assessments show what progress students have made in their learning. Although tutors are not usually involved in selecting these assessments, they may be asked to administer them (after receiving proper training). Tutors may also find it helpful to know which assessments are used by their programs.

In order to get funding, many adult education programs in the United States must show student progress through assessments approved by the National Reporting System (NRS; **http://www.nrsweb.org**). The NRS approves tests for use in ESL program assessment efforts. At the time of this book's publication, approved assessments included the following:

BEST (Basic English Skills Test) Literacy and BEST Plus are available from the Center for Applied Linguistics (**http://www.cal.org/aea**).

Tests of Adult Basic Education Complete Language Assessment System—English (TABE/CLAS–E) are available from CTB/McGraw-Hill (**http://www.ctb.com**).

Comprehensive Adult Student Assessment Systems (CASAS) (**http://www.casas.org**) can be used for all CASAS tests listed below:

- Employability Competency System (ECS) Reading Assessments—Workforce Learning Systems (WLS)
- Functional Writing Assessments
- Employability Competency System (ECS) Listening Assessments—Life Skills (LS)

Currently approved tests are listed on the NRS website.

You can find additional resources related to assessment of adult ESL students by searching the Internet using phrases such as "adult ESL assessment."

For more ideas on how to assess your students, please see Chapter 4 of this book.